FREE

At

Last

By
Halina Cleland
with
Sheila Hollands

1st Printing 20,000 - 2002
2nd Printing 10,000 - 2004
Copyright - © The Master's Foundation

ISBN 1-895918-10-3

Published by: The Master's Foundation
             1290 Eglinton Avenue East, Suite 5
             Mississauga, Ontario, Canada
             L4W 1K8

             Ernie Hollands–Hebron Ministries Inc.
             P.O. Box 1505
             London, Ontario, Canada
             N6A 5M2

CONTENTS

FOREWORD

HOOKED - I am sure some of you have read this book. It is the life story of Ernie Hollands, who spent 25 years in prisons across Canada and the United States of America.

This book has brought HOPE to many inmates around the world, and can now be read in ENGLISH–500,000, RUSSIAN–110,000, CHINESE,–5,000, SPANISH–26,000, and LITHUANIAN–5,000 copies.

I was privileged to be part of the team, as Ernie's wife. While Ernie was traveling and sharing his life story in churches, schools and Full Gospel Business Men's Chapters and Prisons, I took care of his schedule and cared for the inmate correspondence, while raising our family.

In 1991, I initiated and together we promoted, the production of **PRISON CHAINS BROKEN**–60,000 copies. This book contained the life stories of six Canadian ex-inmates whose lives had been changed into productive citizens. Later, it was translated into FRENCH–**CHAINES BRISEES**–10,000 copies and BRAILLE for the blind.

Since Ernie's death in 1996, I have continued to correspond with inmates under ERNIE HOLLANDS HEBRON MINISTRIES INC. To remain relevant and to meet the needs of the inmates of a different decade, God impressed me that this book, FREE AT LAST needed to become a reality. I trust and pray that the life stories of Harold, Dave, Karen, Bob, Gerry and Allan speak HOPE, PEACE & LOVE into your life.

May you experience **INNER FREEDOM** whether you are "inside" or "out" in society.

Sheila Hollands

INTRODUCTION

Read this book! It takes you on a journey of pain, hurt, shattered dreams, broken promises, crime and despair. Then it takes you out of despair into the rebuilding of lives because of God's amazing grace and the deep caring of the community of believers.

For the last thirty years, I have had the privilege of working with prisoners within the Correctional Service Canada. I have found that to become acquainted with prisons is to become acquainted with the many faces of evil and its terrible consequences. However, to become acquainted with Harold, Dave, Karen, Bob, Gerry and Allan is to become acquainted with the fact that despite the detours, the setbacks, and the struggles to be faithful, darkness cannot overcome the light of Christ (John 1:5). Dietrich Bonhoeffer warned about 'cheap grace'. These stories are not about 'cheap grace' but about the cost of discipleship.

I often meet people who are skeptical about conversions among offenders, drug addicts, and street people. I find that it is true that both inside and outside some faith commitments are not taken as seriously as they should be. But I always encourage people to be patient and to 'judge a tree by its' fruit' (Matthew 12:33). A jail conversion should not carry any special privileges for early parole, but you can count on the fact than an authentic conversion will lead to change in attitude towards authority figures, correctional workers and towards oneself. The change will be noted and it might well lead to more positive recommendations on the part of the parole office. Earlier parole should never be the direct result of a faith commitment but it sure can be a logical by-product.

What I appreciate most about the personal stories in this book is the inherent lack of pretense. There is clear acknowledgement of the harm these people caused to others and themselves. There is clear affirmation that when they cried to the Lord out of their depths, He answered them and began walking with them on their path to restoration. The people in the book are real. They do not minimize the difficulties of learning to be a disciple of Jesus. There are still deep valleys, but they do not walk in them alone.

It has been a personal joy to observe their growth and dedication. One parole officer was recently telling me what a pleasure it is to supervise and work with one of the men featured here. He added: "I have a lot of respect for him. I consider him a friend, now, because of his work in the community, a colleague in making the community where we both live a better and safer place to be." This is quite a statement and it could have been made about any of the six people in the book.

Through the years, I have been struck by the boldness of Ephesians 4:28 which, paraphrased, states: Stop your life of crime and do something useful to help others. This is one of the main characteristics of this book. Harold, Dave, Karen, Bob, Gerry and Allan have not only turned their back on a life of crime, lies and addictions, they are now, all of them, doing something very useful to help others. They are doing beautiful things for God in their own communities. I admire their determination to let the light of Christ shine through their brokenness.

As these stories inspire you, may you join me in thanking God for them. May we also be "confident that He who began a good work in them, will carry it on to completion until the day of Christ Jesus' (Philippians 1:6),

The Reverend Doctor Pierre Allard,
Assistant Commissioner,
Community Engagement Correctional Service Canada
and President, International Prison Chaplains' Association

1967 - 2nd Foster Home –
Rosemary, Donnie, Harold.

My Nightmare on Elm Street

The Life
of
Harold Shea

The year was 1980 and I was coming to the end of my rope. It had turned into a nine and a half month run on drugs (LSD), gambling and armed robberies. There was a Nation Wide Warrant out for my arrest. I was on the lam from Toronto to Halifax, Nova Scotia. I wasn't going back to prison this time! They wouldn't take me alive. They'd had me in their custody three times, but due to my alias names I walked again. If they had taken my fingerprints, I would have gone down hard because I was on mandatory parole and still doing robberies.

Now I was sitting in the bathroom at Como's Tavern in Halifax, just across the road from the Strathcona Military Base. In a shopping bag across my lap was a sawed-off shotgun, a Bowie hunting knife, a roll of fiberglass tape, gloves, and a nylon stocking for a mask. Six additional shotgun shells were inside my left shirt pocket. I was ready for business.

When the tavern closed, I would take all the money from the owner and the bartender, who stayed behind and helped the manager close up and do the night deposit. After all, for two weeks I had been staking out this tavern to hold-up and anticipated $25,000 to $40,000 would be mine soon. I planned to have the bartender tape up the manager. I would tape up the bartender and walk away with the loot.

So on July 17, 1980, I was sitting in the bathroom at 11:00 p.m., waiting for closing. It seemed like a long time till 1:00 a.m. The only thing between me and my payday were my two opponents. I reasoned that they would cooperate or go down. I sat wondering if there were any reasons why I shouldn't commit the crime. Each time I came up empty-handed. I needed that money.

If I didn't follow through, I would be sleeping at the Salvation Army or out in the cold. I might go hungry or not be able to play poker and live high on the hog! Each time I did an armed robbery, I would sit and ponder the why's and why not's.

The time was near. I looked at my watch and it was 12:55 a.m. and all appeared well. My intention was to have both men tied up, but those comforting thoughts of non-violence were about to change. Someone tried the door to my cubicle and I didn't respond, so he went into the next cubicle and looked down at me. I pointed the shotgun at his head and told him to get out before I blew his head off. He jumped down and ran out into the bar area yelling, "there's a man in there with a gun". I was furious because my plans were being messed up after two hours of sitting in a stink hole.

Soon I was confronted by twelve angry men, I knew it was time to put up or shut up. All I wanted to do was get out of there. I screamed with all my voice to make the people move back. These men were slowly moving out of the wash-room. One man didn't quite make it through the door when I got to it, so I told him to get down on his hands and knees and start praying or I'd blow his head off. He did as he was told. As I stood there with the single gauge loaded shotgun yelling, I was watching the expressions of those angry men, and I knew they wanted a piece of my hide.

I forgot about the man on the bathroom floor when out of nowhere I felt hands yanking on me. I pulled the trigger and the man behind me pulled back with greater force. The shotgun went off in the air and debris from the ceiling fell on all of us. Then an all out struggle began between bouncers, waiters and myself. I had beaten three men to the floor with the shotgun. Then I began to protect myself with my fists.

2

Next I heard someone yelling, "grab the baseball bats". I looked around wondering where they were coming from, and how I could get out in a hurry. A man about 6'6" approached me like a wild man and started beating my skull with the bat. I counted seven to nine hits and then fell to the floor to protect myself. One man picked up my head and kicked me in both eyes with his cowboy boots. Another smashed back with three swings of his bat.

By the time the ambulance arrived, I had lost half of my blood and my desire to live. When I was placed in the ambulance the last thing I heard was, "don't fall asleep". It was too late. I passed out for two and a half minutes. Why should these ambulance drivers care if I lived or died? I was laying in the back of an ambulance maybe dying and the scariest thing of all was I didn't care. The ambulance drivers revived me as we arrived at Queen Elizabeth Hospital in Halifax. I heard the attendant say, "he's back".

They rushed me into the Emergency Room expecting brain damage and skull fractures because of the blows to my head. I waited almost eleven hours for a specialist to come and X-ray my skull. The doctor on call was very concerned as to why he couldn't get hold of anyone. It was the middle of July and I expect all the specialists were enjoying the weekend or holidays.

Here I was sitting in a wheel chair surrounded by eight police officers. They got my name and date of birth. Soon they came back with my RCMP profile. They cautioned the officers to keep their eyes open because I was dangerous and should not be let out of their sight. I was half dead, why were they concerned about me running away.

The specialist arrived the next morning. My head was examined and X-rayed. I was then taken to another room where I was chained to a stretcher and the police waited outside the door. I could see the specialist talking to another doctor. They were looking at me and shaking their heads. When they came over to me I asked how serious was it and they replied, "that's just it, with the blows to your skull you should have had a number of fractures but there's none". However, over the next two months, I lost the peripheral vision in both eyes and my memory from the age of 13 down, due to the beating. It took over two years to restore my mind and memory.

I was taken to the police station where they took over 12 pictures of my head for evidence in court. They didn't know what to do with my blood-covered coat, so I asked if I could use it for a pillow, because my head was really sore and there were no pillows, blankets or mattress in the cell. There was only a concrete block formed in the shape of a bed. They said okay and I was grateful.

Three days later, I was escorted by two police cars to the Lower Sackville Correctional Institution. I had been there three years earlier facing two counts of armed robbery. I was sentenced to five years at Dorchester Penitentiary. When I arrived I was taken to Administration where Deputy Crowl told me that I should sign my waiver because I wouldn't like my stay if I was there for the full thirty days. He wanted to send me back to Dorchester in the morning.

Why had I become this robber? It all went back to Bloomfield, Prince Edward Island. Lewis Jones, Mom's cousin, lived between us and Keith Prat's store. There was a big field joining us. My brothers, Donnie, Lawrence and myself were using our general strategy in the store. One of us would occupy Mr. Prat, while the other two would shove cookies or candy into our mouths and pockets. We were from a family of ten with little food in the house. At times, we lined up, looking over the shoulder of the one in front, waiting to see if a pancake was left for the last one in line. We were often hungry and had to wait for the next meal to see if we would qualify to eat. We stole to survive.

I was the one who went through my childhood years without boots. This led to a cold, bitter day in January, 1964 when my Aunt and Grandmother reported to social workers, that they had found me with black, frost-bitten feet. I was hospitalized for two weeks and they were concerned that I would lose my foot. My Grandmother came to visit me in the hospital bringing me bags of pink chicken bone candy.

Our father, John Frederick Harold Shea struggled between moonshine and other forms of alcohol, like his father before him. My grandfather, Harold Shea was a hard worker and drove his son to limits and expectations he couldn't live up to. My grandfather had a fishing boat and farm. He employed six to eight people during the Great Depression.

While I was still in my mother's belly, my grandfather was being abusive to his wife, my grandmother, Helen.

Helen decided to take her children and split from PEI and go to Moncton, NB. While she was gone, my grandfather found it lonely, so he phoned and asked her to come back. After she turned him down many times, my grandfather gave up. He went upstairs held his shotgun to his chest and pulled the trigger. My great-aunt Mildred and cousin Ed were outside milking the cows when they heard the shot. They ran to the house and found him dead. Although I was two months into my mother's belly, I am sure that it had a lasting impact on me through my mother's emotions. I know it deeply impacted my father who probably never had a chance to unload his hurts and make amends with his father.

My grandfather gave my father two houses and he sold them from under us to feed his alcohol addiction. Although I wasn't being abused by my father, I did feel abandoned. He would be gone days at a time and no-one knew where he was. My mother had 12 children before she turned 32. I was number five.

Many times the RCMP would drive near our property and roll the old man out of the cruiser into a nearby ditch. My mom and brothers and sisters would drag him out of the ditch. I'm sure Dad made a number of enemies. One day a man dressed in black and driving a black sedan walked up to our door. He started hacking at our door with a hatchet. We were frightened, and our father was nowhere to be found. We rushed out the back door, across the field to mom's cousin and hid there till the stranger left.

Our mother often warned us of threats by the police and/or welfare that they would take us away and split up the family. I was scared because I didn't want my family split up. Like other kids at age seven, I'd take my wooden sword and fight them off. They wouldn't take us alive. I would often sit in my bedroom, where five of us shared the same bed in our two-bedroom house, and I'd talk to my little leprechaun friend. He was my buddy and he understood and comforted me when I had a pain in my heart.

On January 29, 1965, when we were in Mr. Prat's store doing our little scheme, I noticed four plain sedan cars drive by at a slow pace. I panicked and said the police and welfare

5

people are here to take us away. I ran out of the store and across the field. One of the police officers had seen me and chased after me. My little legs couldn't keep up and the next thing I knew he was on top of me.

As I cried hysterically, we were made to say good-bye to Mom. We were promised we could return when Mom and Dad got it together. I stood up in the police cruiser with Donnie and Rosemary and wept. I wondered if I would ever see her again. How could life be so cruel to little children?

We stayed overnight at the Linkletter Motel on Granville Street in Summerside, PEI. Linda, our sister, who was in another room at the hotel, had tried to find a way out during the night, but it was impossible with all the security present. The next day, we were separated and taken to different foster homes.

On February 1, 1965, Donnie, Rosemary and I walked into our nightmare on Elm Street. The social workers taking us to the home assured us that it was a lovely home and how the couple wanted children to love and to help.

When the doors closed behind the social workers, the foster mother, Mrs. M. lined us up against the wall and said, "don't get close to this home because as soon as the bills are paid, you're leaving". Panic and fear gripped our hearts and we knew by the look in her eyes that we were sentenced to hell on earth. We talked of how we would escape from this evil woman.

Every day we hoped that our parents would redeem us and we'd be reunited at home. We were extremely poor before, but I don't remember ever living in such a cruel environment as this foster home.

I recall two occasions when welfare workers came to visit. They'd leave us with a quarter or a couple of little oranges. When they left, Mrs. M. would take them and give them to her two children. She told us that while we were there we wouldn't get any special treatment apart from her children. I guess that explains why she gave her children our oranges.

One day our brother, who was living in a home just two miles away, came to visit us. Mrs. M. had just finished icing a cake and I made the mistake of dragging my finger in the icing to taste it. She hit me across the face with the wooden spoon she was using and broke it. My brother yelled a few words at her and she locked him outside and demanded an apology. I was sent to my room. Rosemary protested and Mrs. M. grabbed her and threw her against a cold cast-iron radiator. She split her head open. They bandaged her up and put her in her room.

In my room, I wondered when this horrible life would end and when we could go home. God? Well I wasn't sure if He was around or even real but I would cry out to Him when I was alone. I often imagined a world where no-one was being hurt and everyone had enough love and food.

Mrs. M.'s son, Frank soon targeted Donnie and me and treated us as though we had invaded his space by living in his home. Frank would shoot us with a bb gun and we would hide under our comforters for cover. If we dared tell our foster parents what Frank was doing, they would beat us and call us liars.

We went to St. Jean's Elementary School, just down the street from the foster home. Our brothers, Stephen and Larry lived with relatives of our foster parents. They were coal miners and worked the boys as slaves while their own children enjoyed casual outings.

At St. Jean's, I met Miss Heinz, one of the nicest human beings a person could meet. She was able to make me feel a bit better about myself and life after the cold treatment I got at the foster home. One thing I really liked in school was the spelling bees, where we would try to outwit one another. Others were amazed by my ability to spell the most difficult words.

The abuse started slowly, a slap here and a hit there. We could never do enough to please these people. Their five year old retarded daughter was another victim of abuse. Mrs M. would wash her in the sink and point out her sexual body parts and explain what they were for. This was obscene and totally gross to us. Before long she was washing our bodies and touching us in private places.

The abuse got worse. We ran away only to be brought back by the police to endure harder beatings. They used belts that were folded in two. They whipped our backs till blood and swellings appeared. We were locked in our bedrooms for days at a time until the swelling disappeared. Mrs. M. told the school we were playing hooky. It was always good to see Miss Heinz again. I think she suspected we were being treated badly at home because she always did nice things for us.

One winter day I saw Miss Heinz across the street in front of the school. I ran across the street to meet her and before I knew it I was in front of a 1965 Valiant car. I went flying through the air and landed on the ground in front of her. The driver came running over and spoke to Miss Heinz. He said maybe I should be taken to hospital and given a big needle. That scared me so I jumped to my feet and showed how well I felt by doing a little dance and then took shelter at Miss Heinz's side.

Often after school, or when we'd play hooky, we'd hang on the back of Irving Oil and Esso trucks to be dragged down the street. We climbed neighbours' sheds that were 10 - 12 feet high. We thought we were invincible. We knew no limits to risk and danger. These were good memories because it took us out of our dysfunctional environment and allowed us to live on the edge.

As I lived at Elm Street, my heart grew cold toward humanity. My heart and my butt became hardened and desensitized to the beatings. Why didn't the police believe our cries for help? Why didn't doctors pick up on our sadness, fearful expressions and suicidal tendencies?

After ten months at the foster home, we were sent to the Arsenaults in Cape Egmont, PEI. They were a nice French Catholic couple who fished and farmed. They were in their mid fifties when they took us in, in 1967. It was nice to get a taste of the country again. The second day at the Arsenaults, my foster mother prepared the water and asked me to take a bath. So I went and got into the bathtub with all my clothes on. Mrs. A couldn't believe her eyes. I had never taken a bath alone before. Here I was at eight and a half taking my first bath.

The Arsenaults showed love, acceptance and stability. The problem was that I was wild and unable to trust anyone. My nightmare on Elm Street had made me a survivor. However, I was blending in as well as I could.

Two weeks after arriving, Mrs. A embraced me and said in her soft, tender voice, "Harold if you are unhappy here, we can find you another home". I remember a tear trickled down my cheek. I wanted to trust but hate raised its' ugly head. The Arsenaults brought in a child specialist to see why we were so distant and unable to adapt to a normal family. When I was asked to draw my feelings about things, the doctor thought I was a bit morbid. I would draw pictures like policemen taking us away. Then I would draw police cruisers turned over and upside down in a ditch and policemen hanging on trees. I thought I had a right to feel this way because the police had taken us away from our Mom and left us in that horrible place, and when we ran away they brought us back to the Nightmare on Elm Street. It began to seem that things may work out for me in this home after all.

One day, Donnie, Rosemary and I went to do some shopping at the Co-Op in Mount Carmel. When we were done, I decided to do a little shoplifting. I pocketed some b b's and a bag of marbles. We had a five mile walk home and when we arrived we found Mr. A waiting with a lobster lat across his lap. He wanted our side of the story, but he didn't buy into our fairy tales so one by one, we bent across his knee and yelled as the lat found it's target ... our butts.

By our second summer with the Arsenaults things between Donnie and I were worsening. The Arsenaults were aging and we were quite a handful. One of us had to go, so they agreed that it should be me. The next day I was given two dollars by the Arsenaults and then taken away . Once again, like when we were taken away from our Mom, I stood up in the back of the car weeping and waving good-bye. Donnie and Rosemary ran down the lane weeping and waving.

I was taken to the Green family near Summerside. They had four daughters but no sons. I became their new son and brother. I was in the home two days and we went into Summerside to do some shopping. I went to the kid's section and bought a real look-a-like cowboy gun and paid for it with the $2.00 from the Arsenaults. I was a real cowboy now. When I got back home I'd pretend to be John Wayne.

On the way home, I took out the gun and started playing with it. Mrs. Green asked where I had got the gun. I told her that I bought it with the $2.00 the Arsenaults had given me. She called me a liar and slapped me across the face. She told me that when we got home, she was calling welfare and having me taken away. I felt stripped again. The rest of the weekend I played outside behind big rolls of hay and pretended that the Greens were the enemy. For the first time in a long time I was telling the truth and was still perceived to be a liar, so I didn't care.

My heart began to pound when we neared Elm Street. I was heading back to my nightmare and this time alone. I wondered what was in store for me this time. I asked God what did I do to deserve a second dose of this medicine. I searched my heart over and over. I wished I hadn't done bad things at the Arsenaults. I would be a better boy if I could go back there right now.

Shortly after returning to Elm Street, I went back to St. Jean's and reunited with old friends from a year and a half earlier. My two older brothers were still attending there and others I knew from my old neighbourhood.

Although things lightened up a bit with Frank, the parents were still very edgy and I didn't dare step out of line. A few months after returning, the M's son and daughter-in-law (who was expecting) came to visit with their children. One night after the son's wife had gone to bed, he came in to where Frank and I were sharing a bed and threw a pitcher of water on us. Frank jumped up swearing and went down stairs. The older brother forced me into sex, then gave me $2.00 to go to the carnival and to keep quiet about the incident. For the next several weeks, I walked around the City of Charlottetown in a daze, feeling dirty.

Following the abuse and the initial shock that my body was experiencing from the intrusion and violation, I went into a new mall. As I was wandering, I noticed a mother and her friend arguing about something, while the baby in the stroller was crying its' heart out. I honestly thought the baby was being abused or neglected, so I ran over and took off with the baby. I ended up at the potato wharf and sat and talked to the baby all day. The baby would cry hysterically and I didn't know how to help it. I picked potatoes off the ground, spit washed them and then tried feeding it to the the baby. The baby would spit it out and reject my idea of food.

At dark, I began to feel hungry and I was at my wits end as to what to do with the child. Two thoughts came to mind. The first was to throw the child into the water. The second was to go up to a nearby park and leave it there. Thank God I acted on the latter. In the park was a police officer on foot patrol. I decided to give the policeman the child. He was about to take my name. I told him I had found the baby near the potato warehouse at the wharf and took off.

The abuse from Frank started again and things began to take their toll on me. Running away became the norm. Many nights I slept in coal sheds near the wharf, or under the church steps. When I was running, I would often eat cow corn or vegetables from farmers' fields. Sometimes I'd go to my brother Larry's foster home. He'd throw down a rope ladder and I'd climb up and sleep under his bed. Another brother would sneak food for me. Other times I'd run away to Cape Egmont Bay and visit Rosemary and Donnie. On two occasions, I was able to arrive at their home and the Arsenaults were amazed that I could get there on my own.

One day after running away, I ran into an old man hunched over, wearing a trench coat and a twenties-style hat. He saw me on the streets and reached out, put his arm on my shoulder and whispered "Jesus loves you". Then he'd put a small leaflet from the Bible into my hand. I walked away confused about who Jesus was, and why He would love me. This happened four times. The fourth time, I asked him his name and where he lived. He gave me his name and told me he lived at the hotel for seniors on Fitzroy Street. Two weeks later I went to say hi and when I got there and described the man, the person told me that no-one matching his description lived there. (I forgot about this old man for 18 years till I became a Christian in Dorchester Prison in 1981).

Another time while on the run from the foster home, I was picked up by the Charlottetown City Police and taken to the Police Station. They asked why I kept running away. I wrapped myself in this wooden chair with my arms and legs around it. The only way I would be free was if someone broke my arms and legs. A police officer asked if I would like to go to his home for the weekend. He said he would find me a new home the first of the week. I wasn't sure if I could trust him but when I thought it possible, I agreed to his deal. He called his wife Diane, and ran everything by her. Then I unwrapped myself from the chair. I got in the back of the police cruiser and was taken back to my Nightmare on Elm Street. I searched my heart as to what had happened between the police officer and myself. He looked so trustworthy and I believed him. Now I knew the police couldn't be trusted. When I got back I was beaten severely and sent to my room for three days with no food.

In April 1968, I stole a truck that was parked nearby. I knew enough to shift to 'D' for drive and then step on the gas, after all I was nine years old and big enough to drive, or so I thought. I drove nine blocks and ran into vehicles. A man ran up to where I was and opened the driver's door. He told the police that he thought a drunk had fallen asleep behind the wheel. After he took me to the police station, he asked if he could take me home for supper and then he'd return me to Elm Street. The police knew the man and his family. He was a fireman who wanted to find out why I was getting into so much trouble, and he invited me to his place for Christmas supper.

A few days later I was brought into Family Court and sentenced to one year at NBTS (New Brunswick Training School). Being labeled incorrigible was not too far from the truth. On April 24, 1968, I was the second youngest child to enter NBTS at the age of 9 years and 10 months. Normally, a person would have to be at least 12 years old to enter NBTS. The reform school was similar to an old army barracks, cold and barren.

Once through Administration, they took me to get a bag of clothes. I was taken to the Mess Hall where I was fed. Finally I was taken to a dormitory and given a bed in an open area where there were seven other beds. I was warned to sleep facing the wall because other boys would come and stick their penises in your mouth while you were sleeping. This scared me and I was determined to stay awake at night and try to sleep during the day.

The second day, I was given the lowdown on the guards and inmates, who were not to be trusted, by the other kids. It was getting scarier by the moment. I was so determined to get out of this place that I began digging a hole under the fence. I only let a few people, who I felt I could trust, in on it. If they wanted to come, they could. It took two weeks, then I was ready to run. No-one else wanted to come because they felt we'd get caught, and besides there was no place to go.

I got through the hole under the fence and my feet were up and running. I kept saying, "feet don't fail me now". I was free. I ran under culverts and through water in fields below the NBTS. I got as far as Mactaquac Dam and then I didn't know which direction to go. Darkness was fast approaching. I tried to catch a fish in a nearby pond. Then I saw a police cruiser coming down the road. I knew they were coming to get me. I didn't bother running because, at my age, where could I go without getting caught.

The police put me in the back of the old police car and took me back to NBTS. They asked if I would like an ice cream and I happily accepted. They asked me questions about why I kept running away. I explained that there were so many people being hurt in that place and I didn't want to go back. They listened, allowed me to finish my cone and then took me back.

When I got back, I was made to kneel in the corner of my dormitory for a long time. I couldn't wait for another chance to run. The next time I would run would be when we were on a field trip. Our field trips were outings into town to go bowling or to a movie.

A couple of months after entering Kingsclear or NBTS, I was playing basketball. When everyone was ready to leave I was asked to stay behind by one of the gym staff. He locked the gym door and asked me to come into the shower room where the lockers were. I wasn't sure what he wanted. All I knew was that I should keep my eyes open. He was the man and I had to obey his commands or I'd be punished. I don't think anything could have prepared me for what was ahead of me. He hurt me in a way that would give me a horrible impression of adults for years to come. He sexually abused me which made me feel dirty inside, just as I felt when Mrs. M's son or son-in-law abused me.

The abuse continued for the next three years and I wandered further into sin and shame of my body and myself. Many other kids there were also victims of abuse at the hands of staff members who had sick fantasies they acted out on children. At night we'd awaken and find other kids doing all kinds of sick jokes to torment the other kids. I would put a

13

rock or stick under my pillow so I could defend myself and beat off stalkers during the night.

Some nights, this guard would work the night shift as a favour to his friends. We would be sexual targets those nights. We returned to society as hard core criminals, ready to strike back with a vengeance. After this time at N.B.T.S., I had been released to a foster home in Darlington NB. They were good, kind, loving people named Bill and Evangeline Phillips. They were Evangelical church people. However Bill was dying of cancer. After his death in the spring of 1971, I returned to N.B.T.S.

One day out of nowhere, I got a phone call from my father. He asked me to describe myself to him. He described himself to me. He said, " I love you son and I've missed you very much over these past seven years, but your mother and I are glad you are coming home." Dad told me that Stephen, Shirley-Ann, Tony, Linda and Lawrence were living with him and Mom. I was so excited, brothers and sisters again! I had just turned 13. Dad told me that on Saturday, I would be coming to Toronto to live with him and the family. I was so happy. The next day I went to school and told my teachers that I was going home. I began to give away some of my inside valuables to my friends.

The next day, April 21, 1971, around mid afternoon, a guard came to me and said my CO, {Classification Officer} Mr. McCarty wanted to see me. Mr. McCarty said, "Come in Harold I need to give you some important news!" I was anxious. Something about his look disturbed me. "Harold, I have some bad news. It is not easy for me to say it!" "Go ahead!" I said! I thought he was going to tell me that I wasn't going to live with my father and mother. He said, "Harold, your father died last night." "You're lying," I screamed at him. I stood up and turned his desk over, and ran out of his office.

Half way down the big hall after trying several door handles, I found a door that was open and went inside and locked myself in. It was a janitor's room. I just sat in the dark for three hours till they found me. They took me to the infirmary where nurses looked after me for the rest of the day and night. I was angry with God. He took my dad away from me. I was told that on Saturday, April 24, 1971 I would be meeting my family on Prince Edward Island. My father's body was being shipped from Toronto by train for the funeral.

As I was driven to the Island, I wondered what my family was like. Will they recognize me? Our car approached Uncle Roy's home. My heart skipped a beat when I saw boys and girls sitting outside on the back steps. They came to greet me. We were all nervous. There were so many children and they all resembled me in some way. One by one they told me who they were and we compared ages. Here it was seven years later and we were reunited. It was a sad occasion but we were just so happy to see each other.

My mother was inside the house with Uncle Roy and Aunt Margaret. I walked towards her not knowing what to say. When she saw me her eyes filled with tears and she smiled. Mom kissed and held me tight and said, "Hello son I'm your mom and I missed you so much". I felt good for the first time in a long time. I was around my family. We went to the funeral home. Donnie, Larry and I clowned around outside. It was a sad occasion but to be reunited was so good. Inside the funeral home, I heard someone say, "he looks so much like his father, Johnny". I got to the front where the coffin was. Mom seemed to be waiting for a reaction from me. I began to dig and pinch my arm so she could see me weep. Would the day ever come when I'd be able to feel again?

After my father's funeral, I returned to Toronto with Stephen, Larry, Mom, Linda, Shirley Ann and Tony. After two days of driving, we arrived at Brooklyn Avenue. I went about from room to room seeing how my family members lived. I noticed the kitchen cupboards were full of groceries. I could see that the old man took care of the practical needs. Things had changed since the mid sixties in PEI. I tried to embrace what it may have been like living as a family, but I couldn't put the pieces together.

I was glad to be with family but was unprepared to encounter the brokenness in the lives of our family members. After four months, Larry and I decided that we'd had enough. We "borrowed" $80.00 from Mom's wallet and headed for PEI.

On PEI, Larry and I met some relatives and stayed at their home. Mom and the other family members came to PEI and we all reunited at Aunt Liz and Uncle George's place. We were scared out of our wits since we'd used mom's money. She reassured us of how much she loved us and told us that the money was replaceable. We still refused to go back to Toronto.

I was placed in another foster home and Larry in a different one. One day when I ran into him he told me he met with a singer-songwriter a few times and we visited his home. His name was Gene MacLellan. He wrote songs that were recorded by Anne Murray, especially her big hit "Snowbird". I told Larry that I didn't believe him and he said that he would prove it to me and he did.

We went out to Gene's home in Pleasant Valley on a number of occasions and stayed there a few nights at a time. Gene was a humble man and would allow us to come back stage. He would introduce us as his friends. This always gave us a lift.

By now, child services on PEI were running out of foster-care homes in which to place us, so they came up with the solution to send us to a place called Sherwood Home. This was a residence for retarded children. We weren't retarded, just plain bad. The Director of the Home grew concerned about my behaviour, of provoking patients, and had me put in a padlocked cell at Riverside Hospital.

Another time, when Larry and I ran away, we walked for about two days with nothing to eat but farmer's veggies and spring water from streams. It was a very hot day and we were hitchhiking on the highway. From within me, I asked God to give us $5.00 so we could go and buy something to eat. We took another 8-10 steps and, as God is my witness, there was $5.00 under a rock. This astounded me and I told Larry about my prayer. We went to a Texaco Service Station and bought, chips, chocolate bars and pop. Maybe there was a God who cared?

Sherwood Home could no longer contain me. The family courts sent me to a reform school until I turned 16 years of age. The offense was stepping on a Canadian flag. I was sent to Shelburne, Nova Scotia School for Boys (NSSB).

Shortly after turning 16, I was picked up and placed in Summerside Jail for two months on 18 break and enters. A few months later, my brother Stephen and I, were charged for breaking into the Wellington Legion. I was sentenced to two years at Dorchester Prison. I was sixteen and a half and fearful of entering the federal prison system because of the rumours I had heard.

At Dorchester, I lived on ' C' side in the old dome and worked in the tailor shop making prisoner clothes. The sad thing about all this was, that I didn't mind doing time because I was used to being institutionalized, from spending six years between reform school and jail to date. A quarter of the guys from Reform School were in prison in Dorchester. I was home.

Shortly after entering prison, I began to act up, drink homemade brew {alcohol} and sniff lacquer and thinners, anything to stay high and blot out painful memories. Segregation and the hole became my second home. I stayed four months over my first prison sentence because of lost remission, that I had accumulated from doing dead time in the hole. In prison I also developed a gambling habit playing poker. This became my obsession over the next several years and the reason for many armed robberies.

I was sent to Carlton Center, a halfway house in Halifax, Nova Scotia. I met some well-organized criminals there. I wanted the recognition of being with these cons. Gambling was the sickest of all diseases to me. I would do almost anything to play poker and to be around fellow criminals or what we liked to be called, the "Cons".

One night George and I were out test running a Charger with hot license plates. We were speeding down Robbie Street in Halifax. Out of nowhere, RCMP cherry roof lights were flashing, so we pulled over. I had a 22 semi automatic on me but didn't have time to throw it out the window. I saw a brown paper bag down by my feet and put the gun into it. Then I stuck it under the seat. The RCMP officers took George into their car and I waited in the Charger. A few minutes later the RCMP officer came over to the car and shone his flashlight around the inside. We made small talk and then he returned to the cruiser. I took my gun out and stuck it down the inside of my belt. I waited another five minutes and then went over to the cruiser and asked the officer how much longer it would be, because I had to get home to the wife and kids. (I wasn't really married, this was just a brush-over to try and rush the officers so we could get out of this predicament).

He told me to get into the back because they were impounding the car.

I got in the back seat next to George and when the police were driving away I pointed down to my gun and made a suggestion to George that we shoot both officers through the wire mesh separating us. George shook his head "no" with amazement on his face. He was stunned that I had a loaded semi automatic on me. If George had told me to go for it I probably would have shot both officers at point blank range.

We got out near Second Street because I didn't live far from there and I didn't want the officers to know my real name or where I lived. After nine and a half months on the run; living under three different assumed aliases; doing 8-10 hits of purple micro dot acid and comic strip blotter, I arrived on July 18th, 1980, at Como's Tavern. This brought me to my encounter with the "Louisville Slugger" baseball bat beating. I was on my way back to prison.

On July 21,1980, I arrived at Dracula Castle, another name for Dorchester. It seemed like old home week for me when I arrived. Guards and convicts recognized me and made jokes. "Welcome back home Shea! Three hots and a cot; can't keep you away! Oh ya! You are the cook!' Jobs scarce on the outside? We saved your bed for you; what took you so long to return?" My second day back, walking around the prison yard, other cons would come up to me and comment about the baseball bat beating I took. They had heard it on the news, TV and Radio!'

I heard that Gene MacLellan was coming to the Chapel in a week's time to put on a concert. I didn't tell anyone I knew Gene, and had stayed at his home a number of times as a teenager. On Saturday July 28, 10 days after my baseball bat beating, I was heading up to the chapel to see Gene and hear him sing "Snowbird" and "Put Your Hand In The Hand". I didn't know that Gene had surrendered his life to Jesus Christ! In fact, I didn't know what that meant, nor was I religious! I'd had too much abuse in my life. I had committed a serious offense. I was going to be a man and do my time.

I entered the Chapel also known as 'The Upper Room'. I sat in the front row all bandaged and sewn up. The whites of my eyes were still red, and blood from the beating was dried to my head. I couldn't take a shower to wash the blood away because my head was infected. The doctors wanted me to wait until healing took place. I didn't smell like roses either! I was sitting in the front row listening to the singing and staring at Gene and he was staring back at me. I thought to myself, 'He can't recognize me in this state.' At break Gene walked toward me. Amazingly, Gene still recognized me in my messed-up condition.

After the break, we went back to our seats. Someone picked up a Bible and started speaking. I thought to myself, "I don't want to hear this garbage and got up and left". There were over 80 people in the Chapel and I was the only one who left. I went back to my cell and laid on my cot, full of anger because of those old feelings from my reform schools days.

At 4:00 p.m., I returned to the chapel to say good-bye to Gene. I walked by three cons leaning against the railing, watching a famous person get ready to leave. In prison, locked away from the world, one couldn't help wonder why a famous Canadian would want to stop and sing songs and bring words of hope to those who are in prison. I passed by the other cons and headed toward the Upper Room Chapel.

Pierre Allard, Chaplain at Dorchester, was letting Gene out of the Chapel. Gene walked over to me and began to tell me that he loved me, his wife loved me and God loved me. Jesus Christ loved me, and if I gave my life to Christ, I would be a free person, the bars wouldn't mean a thing. I couldn't help thinking, why is he telling me all this. I hoped that the three cons leaning against the railing didn't hear what he was saying. My next thought was the scariest, take Gene, throw him over the railing, and he'll either wake up or land on his head.

I wanted to get out of there and escape everything that was happening to me. I couldn't move a muscle. I tried, but was frozen. Gene finished up by giving me his address and taking mine. He said that he would send me some literature. I went back to my cell thinking, it was all over, and memories of Gene would soon fade away.

Each night I'd lie awake on my cot and envision Gene at the end of it telling me, Jesus loved me, God loved me, give your life to Jesus and you'll be a free man, the circumstances wouldn't mean a thing. This bothered me. I wondered if it was going to end, or how to get rid of the thoughts. Finally after two months, I was forced to relive every sin and wrong I had ever committed, as I opened my life to Jesus.

Every day became new to me. I was hungry for God and His love for me through Jesus Christ. Where had I been all my life? How could I have overlooked His great love for me? He was the answer to all my needs and the father who wouldn't abandon me. He didn't want to misuse my body or me. He became a friend to me in times of great trouble and sorrow. He was now the hope of all my tomorrows.

Dorchester, like all institutions, had its code of ethics. Prison mentality is formed through a secretive lifestyle. Only those who abide by the golden rule, to keep a blind eye and pretend everything was okay, were able to co-exist. If you were considered weak, then tougher prisoners would zoom in on you as prey. My mind was torn and stripped from LSD, drugs, and hard living. My secret fantasy was to live and die like John Dillinger, Pretty Boy Floyd or some other famous criminal.

Shortly after entering Dorchester for my fourth prison term, Big Al my previous prison partner suggested that I put in for the Ontario Region Prison System, as I wouldn't enjoy doing time any longer at DP.

The institution was going through some unrest and there were some battles amongst the prisoners and some guards. I had only been back two weeks when trouble broke out on my cell block in B7. Two prisoners began fighting. Five other prisoners and I were locked in on the range when other guards saw the play going on. I broke a leg off a table to defend my fellow brothers should it come down between the man and us convicts.

Shortly after the fight broke out, a task force of guards came in from the B7 tunnel in the old dome and marched us back to our cells. They took out the wounded prisoner. Outside, in the courtyard that day, there were another six fights and the prison immediately suffered a lock down to try and put an end to the violence.

Bill was a Christian guard who had been taken hostage and suffered a knife wound. Later a guard fired a warning shot which accidentally ended Bill's life. One of the most puzzling things that happened during the hostage taking was when Bill requested a Bible. This spoke volumes to me. The four-month lock-down was God ordained. It gave me time to seek God's face and read His word.

During this time at Dorchester, I heard of a former convict returning to the prisons. His name was Ernie Hollands. He was becoming a legend in the system. He smoothed the way for other former convicts and ex-prisoners to follow in his footsteps. Ernie had spent 25 years in prison and could identify with prisoners. He had robbed several banks and escaped prison a number of times, so this made him an icon. If God could change the likes of Ernie, then he could reach countless others through his testimony.

I requested a visit with Ernie prior to his coming into Dorchester Penitentiary. Rev. Pierre Allard sent guards to get me from segregation to visit with him. It was encouraging to meet and talk with this man who would intervene a couple of more times in my life. Chaplain Pierre Allard also made a lasting impression in my life. Pierre and his wife Judy and daughters, Sophie and Amy were so instrumental in impacting hundreds of prisoners.

Ten months into my sentence of eleven years, six months and twenty-eight days, I was taken to Halifax on an appeal before the Supreme Court of Nova Scotia. Many prisoners and guards at DP thought I was crazy to appeal my sentence especially back in Nova Scotia, but I knew that God was in my corner now and He would defend me.

I carried my Bible and case notes. I was shackled and handcuffed to a Russian prisoner. Guards made little comments and digs about my faith, and change of heart. It didn't matter anymore what others said because I had a real big God who loved me and died for my sins on Calvary.

I asked the Supreme Court Justices if I could have the body belt cuffs removed so I could look over my notes, because I was defending myself. I expressed to the panel of three judges that I was a changed man and that, upon my release, I wanted to give back to the youth of our society. This made headlines in the region of Halifax. It was printed on the front pages of the Halifax Herald ... "Born-Again Convict changes his life in prison through the teachings of Jesus Christ". That was okay with me, because I was a changed man and I didn't care who laughed or mocked my new life. A few months went by and I got a letter stating that two years were taken off my sentence. I was happy God had intervened on my behalf.

After a year and a half, I was transferred to Ontario and eventually ended up at Collins Bay Institution. It was 1981 and I had been in prison for about 16-18 months now. This time had a whole new meaning. I was attending chapel on a regular basis and sharing with my new brothers and sisters in prison. I enjoyed meeting the volunteers that came and helped in the chapel services.

When I arrived in Collins Bay in 1981, I began writing my mother every few months. At the bottom of the letter I wrote, 'Love your son, Harold'. Mom would respond and write 'Love Mom' at the bottom of her letters. I wondered if I would be able to say the same, in person, if I met her again!

Collins Bay Chapel was often referred to as The Garden of Eden. My first time in the Chapel scared me because I came from Dorchester Penitentiary, where The Upper Room was predominantly Baptist and Roman Catholic. Now inmates were going around hugging one another and so were the outsiders. This also scared me and I asked myself the question, "What if some of these individuals were gay?" I came out of an abusive past and didn't want anyone touching me, so I would walk behind them and go sit down. This lasted for four or five weeks attending chapel.

As time went on, I began to see a sincere heart in these individuals and felt their love was genuine, so I allowed the odd one to hug me. It felt good. It broke barriers in my heart and soul. I spent many hours before my maker, crying out and asking Him to cleanse my soul and make me whole. I asked Jesus what it would be like on the cross, and in my spirit and mind, I would picture Him. What a horrible scene, nothing like I had ever seen in paintings.

There were five evenings in a row that I would go down in the supper parade. Each time I picked up my food and placed it on the tray and began to walk around this brass railing to sit down, an awesome anointing of the Holy Ghost would fall on me. I immediately felt drunk in the Spirit. I didn't know whether to sit, walk or stand. Everyone was looking at me in wonder, but it was okay because the living God was at work in me and it was precious. Nothing could compare to those five wonderful evenings, in HIS presence.

While at Collins Bay, I worked in the laundry room, the kitchen and finally the masonry shop. I learned to lay bricks, mix mortar, and cut angles out that were sketched on the brick. I would also build walls and other things. One day while walking to work, another prisoner and myself were talking about movies and I told him of one I watched the night before. It had a fair amount of violence in it. He asked me, " As a Christian should you be watching such a program?" The thought never entered my mind, but after he asked the question, it bothered me. Maybe I wasn't the example that I should be. I had to do some soul searching over this incident and thanked this individual for opening my eyes.

Another situation happened when I was on the scaffold on the fourth tier. This Italian fellow named Rocco was mouthing off to me. I lost my cool and picked up a 33 pound cement block and threw it at him. Fortunately he ducked and the block smashed up against a forklift behind him. Again I had to go back, humble myself and ask for forgiveness.

Another incident happened when I worked in the kitchen. I was having a bad day, so I went to my cell and slammed the door. Moments later, this individual to whom I had been witnessing, came in and sat on my bed. He asked me some questions. I regained my composure and started to share the gospel with him. He began to try and intimidate me and mock the Bible. I totally lost it and began beating him over the head with my Bible. I told him to get out of my cell and take the devil with him.

When would I learn? I went to the Chapel and spoke with Chaplain Reg Solmes. He prayed with me and I asked both God and the prisoner for forgiveness. Ironically, two weeks later that prisoner gave his heart to the Lord. {I wouldn't suggest this practice to all Christians.}

Peter and Ruth Hennessey were volunteers who had a strong influence in my life. They wrote to me in between meetings and were encouragers on a regular basis. A number of times I went on passes to their tent meetings in Cherry Valley near Picton, Ontario. In Collins Bay they were holding three-day Karios Weekends. I heard so much about them that I signed up. This was when inmates and volunteers would be allowed to stay together in the chapel for a three-day period. I met a lot of wonderful volunteers who made my Karios Weekend special. I met Rev. James Craig who would impact my life. I also met Lou and his wonderful wife, Romaine who was Director of The St. Leonard's Half Way House.

Romaine asked me where I was going when I got out, and I told her I didn't know. She said, "Harold, why don't you come to Sudbury and live in our Christian half-way house?". I didn't want to be rude, but I asked where Sudbury was. She told me where it was and what it was like being a northerner. I thank God for early experiences with stable Christians who spoke into my life. Especially to Gene and Judy and their family, Ernie and Sheila Hollands and their family, Lou and Romaine, James and Susan Craig and their children, Grant and Sarah, their in-laws, Peter and Ruth Hennessey, Jimmy Cavanagh, Darryl Gellner, Brian Bush, Billy Shannon, Bob Lameroux and many others.

After being given a conditional pre-release program for a farm annex, Bath Institution was my next stop. Every three months I was allowed to go to Sudbury to St. Leonard's House.

Bath Institution was a relaxed place with no walls and no fences. When I arrived at Bath, Ontario, the kitchen learned of my baking abilities and asked me to come on board as a baker. I made pastries for both Bath and Millhaven Prison. Cooking was a joy to me since Kingsclear Reform school. Time went by rather well at the Bath Institution. I had my work and I worked out on the weights. Then I was asked to join the inmate committee. I helped the Chaplain with the Gospel Groups and I helped build the outdoor skating rink.

I was asked to go out on a pass to a Full Gospel Business Men's Meeting. They introduced me as the short testimony speaker. Their keynote speaker was Monty Lewis. I thought to myself, "I know a Monty Lewis, but it surely wouldn't be the same person". Monty thought the same thing when he heard my name. Sure enough it was the Monty I knew. I was surprised to see an old prison buddy up in Ontario. I learned that Monty had married a lady named Lynda and now had

Ernie Hollands, Harold Shea, Enoch Kerr, Peter Hennessey

children. He came to visit us at Bath and I looked forward to those visits.

Shortly after this, I went out on passes to Monty and Lynda's home and to their church. In the fall of 1982, I was baptised in water in their Church. After service, we went back to Bill, Susan, Cory and Erwin Eagleson's home and had lunch. I returned to Bath, full of the spirit of God and wanting to find a quiet place to go and dwell in HIS presence, the presence of my maker.

I studied the Word of God with my whole heart. I read the word of faith books by Kenneth Copeland, Kenneth Hagin and Kenneth Kenyon. In 1982, Rev. John Rice came in and interviewed me on his TV program "Broken Pieces". The show was aired in the Kingston region to open the eyes of the community as to what prisoners went through, and how they could overcome obstacles in their lives through Jesus Christ.

Gene MacLellan and Royce Harris were doing an across Canada tour, so I asked Gene if they'd visit me in Bath and they did. I had saved $9.00 and had a personalized wallet made with GENE written on it and I wanted to give it to him before they left. Gene didn't want to take the money, but I insisted.

Gene, his wife Judy and their children, Philip, Catherine and Rachel came and brought me a family picture. On the back they each wrote something about our visit. Monty told me that he had always wanted to meet Gene, so I told him to come on Saturday, December 11, 1982, and he could meet him at the family Christmas party. Prior to my conversion, I'd had only one visit in 13 1/2 years.

My Classification Officer told me in November, that if I could obtain work in Sudbury I would likely make conditional day parole in December 1982. I called Romaine about The Overhead Doors' owner, who mentioned that if I needed employment upon my release to contact him. A week later I got a letter stating, I would have work with The Overhead Door. Word came back to me on the 14th of December 1982, that I was being day paroled to St. Leonard's Half Way House in Sudbury.

Lou and Romaine came down and picked up Neil and myself. This was the best Christmas present I had ever received, to spend Christmas with a good Christian family and to spend time with Pastor Jim and Sue and Grant and Sarah Craig. I was only out a short time when I ran into complications with my Parole Officer and with my newfound Christian Faith.

The job I was promised fell through. My P.O. (Parole Officer) began to put pressure on me about getting employment. It was two months since my release and there was no sign of work through Unemployment Services. I was determined that I was going to find my own work. One day I got a call from Unemployment about a job at Golden Pizza. I went for the interview and was called back for a second one. The owner of the restaurant said that out of 15 applicants, I was the most favourable. These words spoke life into me.

Each night after work, I hitchhiked to Chelmsford to help manage a street ministry called 'The Lighthouse'. It was a street ministry for youth on the street. They could drop in, play games, enjoy soft drinks, listen to Christian bands, and hear testimonies of others, who were set free of drugs and overcame problems in their life by trusting in Christ Jesus as their Lord and friend.

After nine months at Golden Pizza, I went down to Hebron Farm in Indian River, near Peterborough, Ontario to visit with Ernie and Sheila Hollands and their children, Susan, Peter, Robert and little Joy. This was late August to early September 1983. It was a beautiful place designed for ex-cons who wanted to take their walk with Jesus Christ seriously. I was the first ex-con to visit Hebron Farm, two weeks before it opened.

I met with Don and Gladys Woodcock who were the farm parents and ironically, it was God's timing in their lives. They recently lost a son whose birthday was the same as mine, and they saw my coming as a time of healing in their own lives. Hebron Farm was the place I needed to be to have a rest from all the pressure I felt back in Sudbury. The plan I had before coming to the farm was that Gene MacLellan was going to come there and drive me back to Sudbury and Gene was going to sing in The Lighthouse. Gene was also going to sing at my Church, New Life Christian Centre. What a beautiful holiday, Gene and I had a great time renewing our friendship in Christ and sharing gospel truths all the way back to Sudbury.

After being laid off from Golden Pizza, a Catholic, Christian lady, Olive, mentioned to me about cook jobs on train gangs and bush camps. The next day I called Rick . I told him about being an ex-con, if that made a difference. He said half the people working for us are ex-cons because they seem to be able to handle the isolation best. Rick said he'd call in March and April when they were hiring.

Two days later I was lying on my bed at the Half Way House and I said, "God, if you love me, give me a job within three days". As I was praying, I heard the phone ring and someone yelled that the phone was for me. It was Rick and he said, "Hi Harold, are you ready to go to work?" I told him I would call my Parole Officer to see if he'll let me. He gave me a 30 day work travel visa. I called Monty Lewis and told him the good news. Monty cautioned me about the lifestyle in the remote north, and how tough it was being exposed to the alcohol and drugs. I thanked him for his advice.

My first contract was to feed a CN Train Gang in Northern Ontario. Monty was right about the amount of drinking and partying. Next, I took a job in Fraserdale, Ontario as Chef Manager at a logging project. I spent the next six months isolated there. I was lonely. I began to compromise with a drink of Kahlua in my coffee. Next, I joined the foremen in a friendly game of scat, {31} for a dollar a card. This was taking me further away from the voice of my Saviour. Then I began to go along and have an occasional beer with the boys.

The North West Territories were looking for a night baker, meat cutter and cook. I qualified for all three. Little Cornwallis Island was probably the nicest remote site in the world. We had indoor gyms, swimming pools, wet and dry saunas, and green houses. There were two dining rooms and the best food a company cook could dish out, on a cost plus arrangement.

After my six-month stay at Cornwallis I took a little rest before heading to a job position at Nanasivik on Baffin Island, nine miles from the Arctic Bay. Then in October, 1985 while baking at Hemlo, Noranda Site, one of the richest gold bodies in the world, I was carrying two bags of flour, when a pain shot up from my ankle. I was forced to go off work for three months and went to Thunder Bay for physiotherapy.

On returning to Sudbury in January 1986, I was approached to start up a bakery in Chelmsford Ontario. Harold's Bakery was born on a shoestring budget. Four other Christians had loaned me $500 each, to get the bakery up and running. The business was showing signs of success. The previous owner continually increased the rent. By four months, I couldn't handle any more schemes from him. I started dabbling in drugs to keep my fatigued body and mind alert. Church people were encouraged by how well I was doing, but I didn't share my burdens with them. I felt it would discourage them if they knew how I was feeling inside.

One day I called one of my investors and told him I was leaving town for a while to get some sanity, and I wanted him to store all the bakery stock and equipment. He waited for a couple of days. By then, the owner had put a chain on the door. During my travels, I went to eleven cities in six months, running from everything and all those who had grown to love me, trying to find my first love, God. I abandoned my friends as my father did me, so many years earlier.

After the end of my travels, I returned to Sudbury. I had colored my hair and started to hit the booze and drugs again. Then I began fighting at the Zoo {Coulson Hotel, in Sudbury}. One night I came out of May's tavern and asked a cabby if he could cash a hundred dollar bill. He said he could. I got him to drive up the back of Copper Street. This was the lowest I had come in my life. I was desperate for more drugs and this man had the money. Three times I attempted to rob him, but each time the voice would say, "Harold are you doing this in the name of Jesus?" When the cabby learned I didn't have money to pay him, he took me to the police station. My old friend Zoel arrived at 2:40 a.m. with the money and saved me. I gave him the knife I had been carrying. Zoel still jokes with me to this day, that if I want the knife back, he still has it.

I came to London, Ontario and took a job in construction. This was a good job. Each day after work I would go into the Town and Country Restaurant and enjoy their supper special. Occasionally, I would order a beer.

One extremely hot day, I went into an air-conditioned building. When I came out, the sun hit me, I lost my balance and felt dizzy. As I regained my balance, there was an ex-police officer watching who recognized me from my photo in the police files of ex-parolees. He reported me to the John Howard Society. A week later I went to the police station to sign in. I was arrested and taken to Elgin Detention Centre in London. The ex-police officer, a Pentecostal Christian, came to visit me the next day and explained who he was and why he did what he did. It was to help me get back on the path of Christianity.

I ended up going back to Millhaven and then to the Bath Institution, from where I'd been released in 1982. Here it was 1987, and I was going backward in time, because I had left town without a travel permit. It didn't matter at that time. I just wanted some peace and contentment.

In the spring of 1987, Pastor Jim who was a long time friend and encourager in my life, came to visit me with a couple by the name of Bram and Alice Brower. The Brower's owned and operated a Christian resort in Wallaceburg Ontario. After my release, Bluewater Shiloh Park became my home and place of work for the next ten months. Things began to pick up in my life for a while.

In 1988 I got in touch with Ernie and Sheila Hollands and asked for help to get my life back on the straight and narrow. I knew Hebron Farm was a place of refuge. I went to Hebron Farm in Ailsa Craig near London, Ontario. This time at Hebron there were many changes. There were different house parents, and I was a harder case to handle. I stayed for two months and then had to move on.

After two more jobs up north, I asked permission from my Parole Officer to visit my family in PEI and was denied. I decided to go anyway. It was good to see mom and the family. I tried to share my Christian walk with them. No-one seemed too interested in hearing about God. Through rejection, I decided to share in their drinking and started to return to my old ways, fighting again! All hell broke loose at the local biker's after hours' drinking club. I was dragged to the floor and held down by six bikers. Fist after fist landed home and I could feel bones breaking. Outside, I was hit with a brick or a two-by-four and my lower front teeth caved in.

I went to the Hospital. Dr. MacLean was on call that night so he examined me and took X-rays of my facial area. He discovered that I had, both temples broken in two, and my jaw broken in three places. He told me that I needed immediate surgery to reset my jaw, and I should pray that my temples heal normally.

After walking around town for a few days and contemplating going back with weapons to take revenge on those in the club, I decided to go over to Summerside instead and visit my favorite Aunt Sheila and her husband Lorne. After a couple of days Sheila asked me to start reading my Bible again. She said, "Harold, we liked you better when you talked about God and read your Bible". This crushed me, that someone so close to me could directly challenge me. I told her that I didn't think that I could get back into the Bible because I'd been away from God for so long. Sheila said, "Just do it". I went and picked up the Bible and started to read. Silent tears fell and turned into tears of joy. God was speaking to my heart again.

My cousin told me of an evangelist who was speaking at the Linkletter Hotel over the next few days. The evangelist was Monty Lewis. My heart skipped a beat. I told my aunt and cousins that they had to go with me because Monty had an amazing testimony, and he was a personal friend of mine. My Aunt Sheila and cousins John and Trina were uncomfortable hearing about Monty's past, but were awe struck at how God could touch such a man and turn him around. Sheila asked me to invite him over so Lorne could meet him, because Lorne wouldn't believe his story unless he met him in person.

Lorne and Monty kicked it off okay. Monty stayed till nearly midnight and before leaving, prayed with us and especially asked God to keep his hand on me. That night my aunt said, "Harold, why don't you turn yourself in to the law and make things right with God"? I asked, "how do I do that"? She suggested I call a parole office and ask them.

The next day, Tuesday, I called the Moncton Parole Office and asked the secretary who was in charge. She responded, "Jack ". I said, "Jack from Halifax"? She replied, "Yes"! I said, "put me through to him, please"! I told Jack my name. He recognized me immediately. Jack was my counselor eleven years earlier, when I was at the Carlton Centre in Halifax, Nova Scotia. I explained my predicament to Jack and he responded with, "Harold, you can turn yourself in and face going back to the institution for a short while for being out of your area, or you can go on and risk getting into more trouble and going to prison for a longer time". I knew what he was saying was true. I decided to turn myself in.

A week went by rather quickly, but I was reading God's Word and asking His forgiveness for my horrible journey of sin. The night before heading to Moncton I couldn't sleep for fear of the unknown so I got up and made homemade bread for my aunt. The next day I suggested that she just drop me off at the Parole Office. She refused to do that just in case I backed out and went out the back door of the building.

After a half hour of talking, Jack asked me whether I wanted to go to Springhill or Dorchester. I said "Springhill". I also wanted to be close to my brother Donnie, who I hadn't seen in seven years. Within three hours Donnie learned of my being in the institution and came and visited me.

Within three days, the institutional staff heard of my abilities to cook and bake and got me on the kitchen range. My brother Donnie was also a line cook in the kitchen so we ended up on the same range. Donnie came around each night and encouraged me to go to church. After about three weeks, Donnie took me to church. Rev. John Tonks was the institutional Chaplain. It felt good to be back in the house of God! Each day being around Christians I felt stronger. Once again, I developed a desire to seek and serve the master carpenter, Jesus Christ.

Within a couple of weeks of returning to prison, I learned that I would be released on January 3rd.1989. In one way I was excited and in another scared. Scared of going back to nothing and starting over again. I was ashamed that I had let God, and believers who trusted me, down. A few days before Christmas 1988, I knelt by my bed and prayed a simple prayer to God. I said, "God, when I get out in January, either give me a wife or kill me and take me home. God heard my desperate cry. I had made a full circle. It was here I first gave my life to Jesus. I had walked away, now God in His mercy was restoring me.

On January 3rd. 1989, I was released to Cannell House in Moncton NB. I met up with Gary Lands and we hit it off. On my fourth day Gary asked me if I'd like to go over and meet his friend Joan. I was game for this because I didn't know anyone in town and missed the family-style interaction with others.

Joan and her family seemed down to earth. She asked if I'd like to meet her friend, Golda. I agreed. They called her and she came over. Sitting at the kitchen table in Joan's kitchen, I studied Golda and perceived her to be a country style gal who enjoyed children and having her own little nest. We went out for coffee and I apologized that I had just gotten out of prison and didn't have money to buy her a coffee. She said that was okay, that she'd buy the coffee. I told her I'd buy the coffee at a later date. She was okay with that!

A week later we had supper together. About two weeks later, we were talking hypothetically about marriage and questionable roles in the family setting. I brought up the role of Christ in the home and living a Christian lifestyle. Golda informed me that her previous boyfriend of eight years turned to religion, mostly as a crutch, and that turned her off. When she first uttered these words, I was swift to judge. However, I bounced back with a hopeful smile that one day we would be joined in agreement under Christ.

I got a job about three weeks after my release as a night chef at the Colonial Inn on Highfield Street. I began to get well known for my rich thick soups, split pea, and clam and seafood stews. I enjoyed Golda coming down at night and having a seafood salad or a soup. We were becoming good friends and I was forming a true and pure love for her. We walked everywhere we went. We started to become aware of each others strengths and weaknesses.

After a week at work, I noticed a sign in the lobby of the hotel that there was a Full Gospel Business Men's Monthly Meeting being held on Friday night. I asked Golda if she would join me at a special supper and I explained the meeting to her. She was game to give it a try. Friday's FGBMFI's banquet went well and Golda and I both enjoyed the evening. Golda agreed to attend church with me on Sunday. At the end of the service, I suggested Golda and Joan go to the front for prayer. They did and when Golda came walking back down the aisle I could see joy, peace and contentment on her face.

A few more weeks went by and Golda's parents wanted to meet me and invited me for supper. Afterwards Mr. R. invited me to watch the news with him and I asked for his daughter's hand in marriage. He told me she was big enough to make her own decisions but it was okay with him. I took this as a yes and went back upstairs with a smile on my face.

Golda was a live-in nanny. Her boss invited us for supper as they also wanted to meet me. After supper I went and sat down with her boss who was an undercover RCMP officer. He and I didn't say too much and I am sure he picked up the tense feelings we had. The second time over visiting Golda, his wife Michelle asked Golda what my last name was. I told Golda on the way home that evening that he was going to have a security check done on me. Golda said, "If he does, I will quit my job". I insisted that it wasn't necessary and we could meet away from her work so she didn't have to risk her job.

Sure enough, the next day, Brian her boss, talked over the results of my security check with Golda. He asked why she didn't disclose who I was, and that I had a criminal record, especially with the number of cautions on my file. He said, "What if Harold decided to go into our bedroom and take my spare weapon or take our children hostage?" Golda assured him that I was legitimate and not out to hurt him or his family. He wanted to see me. I didn't feel I had to, but decided to go and talk to him because I did enter his home on two occasions. He went over my file and asked about my two occasions of returning to Millhaven and Springhill? He was wondering why I returned if I hadn't committed a crime since 1980. I explained about my two violations of leaving my paroled area.

I received my income tax refund and went out and bought Golda an engagement ring. I gave it to her sitting down near a tree in the High Field Square on St. Patrick's Day. She was delighted. On May 20, 1989, we headed off to Camp Petawawa in the Ottawa Valley. We were hired to run the pastry department for 1,200 to 1,700 cadets and officers.

After eight weeks on this contract, we arrived in Sudbury by train on June 5th. We went to visit the Craig's because we made plans over the phone to have our wedding on June 7th, 1989 as Golda's parents' anniversary was June 7th. We had fifteen people at our wedding. It was very emotional for me and brought tears to my eyes because I never thought this day would come. I thought I would never get married because of

34

all the hurts and intrusions into my life. I never thought that I was good enough for any woman.

On June 10th we headed to Edmonton, Alberta to work. I got a job at CFB Penhold near Red Deer as Chief Baker. We found a nice basement apartment and were able to get into a good church. On May 24 1990, we were happy to help get my brother Donnie out on Parole to come and live with us. Donnie went on to Bible College, and we finished a job in Alaska then returned to Sudbury.

In September, 1991 we attended a Full Gospel Business Men's supper. Bill St. Pierre was the speaker. He was one of the VP's of Circle Square Ranches, which are children's programs across Canada. Bill shared about how so many children and teens were helped through these camps and how they were looking for helpers to work there year round. We visited Circle Square Ranch in Severn Bridge in Washago, Ontario. This would be in late September or early October 1991.

On December 10th, 1991, we received the phone call. We packed everything and brought our six full suitcases and ten large boxes to Severn Bridge. For the next year we lived in a room about 10 x 10 feet. We worked managing the kitchen. It saddened my heart to see so many young people who came from similar but different home environments like myself.

After a year at Circle Square Ranch, Golda and I went back east to spend some quality time with Gene MacLellan in P.E.I. Gene helped us with groceries and getting settled in our apartment. Shortly after moving in Golda and I were watching the news one night and a news clip came on and it went something like this, " In Kingsclear, New Brunswick a previous guard who worked at the New Brunswick Training School was being charged for several accounts of sexual abuse, more to follow after the break".

Without seeing who it was or any names given, I turned to my wife and said, "I bet you his name is __ __". Golda asked, "Why, do you know him?" "Yes" I replied. I will explain more if it is him. After the break my guess was right and they showed his picture. I explained to Golda the hell that I, and many others, endured while at NBTS. A few days later a beep came over our intercom and it was an investigator

Gene and Judy Mac Lellan family – Harold's last visit prior to his release on Dec. 22/80

from NBTS. He told me that other boys from NBTS mentioned that he should see me, as I was one of the worst ones abused in the sixties and early seventies. It was hard reliving those painful memories.

I would talk in bits and pieces to Gene about the investigation. I thank God for the four months that Gene and I were able to spend together. In September, 1992, after four months in PEI, we returned to Ontario and took the chef's job at another Circle Square Ranch in Arden, Ontario. We worked long hours and lived again in a small room setting with all our personal belongings around our bed.

In the fall of 1993, after rounds of talks, Richard, Golda and I agreed to move back to Sudbury and open a farm to help addictive persons come off alcohol and drugs, and turn their lives over to Jesus Christ. This venture failed to become a reality

After two months we found an apartment at 244 Riverside Drive in Sudbury and in the Spring of 1994 Golda and I took on a job working at a children's camp on John Island up near Manatoulin Island two hours from Sudbury.

Good news arrived the summer of 1994. Something I

36

Brandon Gene, Golda, and Harold Shea

wanted my whole life was about to happen. Our son was to be born in February 1995. Our hearts leapt with joy. God was going to bless us with a son, Brandon Gene MacLellan Shea. What a joy! What a honour!

On December 8, 1995, Overcomers of Sudbury was born as eight men and I joined together to reach out to the community with the love of Jesus. We do prison visitation and one-on-one visitation. We minister in the jails and Young Offenders centres. In the first three years of services, over 200 people have decided to know Jesus in a personal relationship. I continue to speak in schools and clubs. We began to develop volunteers to coordinate Twelve Step Overcomers Groups. This weekly program helps those overcome problems due to addictive lifestyles. Today there are over eleven Overcomers Groups in the Sudbury area. Three are in the Cecil Facer Young Offenders Centre. Each year we give Goodie Bags at Christmas and continue with assistance to the needy throughout the year.

In December of 1994, I phoned Gene and learned that he was suffering from a brain tumor. I spent many hours speaking with him on the phone for the next few days. On January 18, 1995, I spoke with Gene for the last time. We attended his funeral and this time I really could cry. I had lost a man I dearly loved. A man who had led me to deep places in God through our Lord Jesus Christ.

During the next year I was attending school, taking computer courses and up-grading at Cambrian College. At age 38 I returned to school. At 40 years of age in 1998, I went to Ontario Business College and did a three year addiction course which was interwoven into one year.

We were approved as Foster Parents, and since 1997 we have had a number of babies, children and teens live in our home. It is good to be making a positive contribution to their lives. Since I have lived in their shoes, I am better able to help them.

In 1999, Pastor Larry Haner of The Valley Pentecostal Church had a special service acknowledging me as an ordained minister, licensed with Gospel Crusades of Canada. Also in 1999, I started my second Diploma in Restorative Justice at Queens Theological College and Queens University in Kingston Ontario. I will graduate in May, 2002.

Restorative Justice was the missing piece of the puzzle to bring balance and comprehension into my life. In my view, Restorative Justice is the motor that is missing in society. It could revolutionize our societies and help families live healthier lifestyles. Restorative Justice challenges us to repair the harm that is done to one another, victim and offender. It is reconciliation through the process of forgiveness. Restorative Justice is truly adaptable for all facets of society, from law enforcement to the clergy, to the average home and to people of all languages and beliefs.

My next dream, which is even now becoming a reality, is to establish a farm in memory of Ernie Holland's and Gene MacLellan, called "Hebron Two". This farm will meet the needs of victims, offenders, and those struggling with addictions. Hebron Two will be a place of rest and restoration.

If God could change me when I finally turned over every area of my life to Him, I challenge you that He can do the same for you. It doesn't matter what hurts or addictions are in your life. God is able.

No prison on the inside or outside is too big or too small that the love of Jesus Christ can't come in and turn on the light. Our God is so big, He can change everything that we hold inside that prevents us from growing in Him. Let Him replace your old ways with His holy ways.

Remember, don't settle for second best, settle for Jesus Christ, God's best for you and I.

Harold Shea
P.O. Box 20074
150 Churchill Blvd.
Sault Ste Marie, ON
P6A 6W3

Wheeling and Dealing

The Life
of
DAVE HARDY

In 1986, I was hospitalized with a blood clot in my leg. I was in a private room so I could smoke. I went into the bathroom and smoked half a joint, then came back to bed. Later on, I felt really strange. I told Karen to call the nurse. All of a sudden my eyes shot back in my head and I began having convulsions. Karen ran into the hall screaming for someone to help. I knew that I had died and began to have an out-of-body experience.

I had a trip of what I believe was my "hell" experience. The next thing I remember was that I was in a place where fire was burning everywhere, although it gave off no light. As I was marveling at the reality of fire without light, I continued moving forward, looking from side to side. It was utter darkness. Out of the darkness coming towards me, I saw two hideous looking entities. Fear gripped my heart like never before. The only thing I could think of doing was calling on Jesus' name. I cried out "Jesus! Jesus! Jesus!" The nurses thought I was swearing, but it was my desperate cry for life not death.

Immediately I found myself back in my hospital room,

but I was in the upper right hand corner near the ceiling. I hovered there for what seems like ages, still engulfed with fear of what I had just experienced. I could see them working on my body with the paddles (electrical defibrillation). Suddenly I spiraled back into my body as my heart began to beat again.

There must be a reason for me to live, even though my earliest beginnings were so confusing.

I was born July 7, 1946 in St. John, NB. to a single mother I never knew and still don't, by the name of Katherine Nickerson. Back then, being a single parent was a disgrace. My father had a relationship with this woman who became pregnant with me. He was married to Ethel Hardy, the only mother I did know. They had no children. My father convinced Katherine to give me up and Ethel to adopt me. My dad must have been quite a talker.

I was adopted at eight days old and raised by the only parents I have ever known. My adoption papers were made up but never signed so I was born Gary Wayne Nickerson to Katherine Nickerson, son of Harold Hardy. Only ten years ago did I change my name legally, to David Hardy. Most of my life I went by two names. My name was changed when I was adopted, so I grew up believing that my mom and dad were my real parents.

I grew up in a rural setting in Sussex, NB around places like Shannon, Henderson Settlement, and Bald Hill. I was an only child. From the time I was three or four years old, my mother took me to church and Sunday School. My father rarely went but read his Bible at home. Many times, he told me things about life that came directly from the Scriptures. My father knew the value of good principles and he taught them to me. I probably went to church until I was about eleven or twelve. I excelled in church. I remember getting certificates for memorizing catechisms and various scriptures in the Bible. I'm thankful for those roots, although there were times I wondered about them.

We were very poor and had to travel around so dad could find work. My father was an unskilled labourer and because work was scarce in the fifties, we moved around a lot. He worked as a farm hand or as a wood worker. He was gone from dawn to dusk. I remember living in Henderson

Settlement. My father was working in the woods around Bald Hill. One day, when I was just a little boy, mom and I were out to the store and dad was working, and someone burned our house down .

We moved back to Hanwell's Settlement near Fredericton in 1950 and lived in the first house we ever owned. It was built by the men in the community and the lumber was supplied as well. Here I started school in a rural one-room school house. Eight grades, one room, one teacher. With only one teacher, the amount of time that could be spent with each student was limited. Fortunately, my parents always spent time with me in my studies at home. When I began school I knew most of the work because I had been taught at home. As a result, I excelled in school. I was a very smart child, and things came easily to me.

The poverty mentality hit me early and created a lot of shyness, shame and reserve in me. I was very introverted. I only ever had hand-me-down clothes. The clothes had holes in them and were usually too big. I was embarrassed to wear them. Today they'd be in fashion.

My first school teacher had a daughter the same age as me. I did well in the early grades and I should have been moved to the next grade. I was held back because the teacher didn't want me to advance past her daughter. Looking back, I believe that changed the course of my history. School work became monotonous.

One Halloween night when we lived in Shannon, I almost choked on a peppermint. Someone had scraped at our window and scared me, leaving me with a fear of the dark. I'd been left in the house on my own while my mother checked on dad.

From there I went to the City of Fredericton for part of a year, in Grade Two. I was seven and it was a different world. There was no one-room school. It was quite a change for me, being so shy and poverty stricken. My father was a commissionaire in the old movie theatre. He wore a commissionaire's uniform and it was the best job he ever had.

I remember the religious conflict in the community. We lived in a Protestant Presbyterian community. People in the church told my mother not to allow me to hang around with the Peterson boys who were Catholics. There were about three Catholic families in our community. I'm thankful that my mother didn't buy into that belief and I grew up with the Petersons. It sounds a little like Ireland but this was the 50's in Fredericton, New Brunswick.

It was my first time in a large school where every grade was separate. It was also my first experience at fighting. I was small, scrawny and intimidated because I was the new kid in school. I was a shy kid and scared of fighting. I would do everything I could to avoid it. I was bullied by the older kids as I tried to win favour in this new school. So, I'd get into fights with the bullies. There was one incident involving a person who continually bullied me and the other kids by throwing us in snow banks and other things. One day he caught me and backed me into a corner. I freaked out. I kicked him in the face to protect myself. To my surprise, I won the fight. I was never bothered by the bully or anyone else again. I wasn't a hero, I was just scared to death and trying to get away.

When my father used to come home in his commissionaire's uniform, the kids thought he was a police officer and took off. One time I got out of a scrape just because of my dad's uniform. I generally got along with other kids. While in Grade 2, we used to play in the rail cars.

I remember being accosted by this guy who was a University student. He paid us each a quarter and did a minimal amount of abuse to us boys. Most of the sexual abuse went on with a young girl. We were made to expose ourselves and watch what went on. A few weeks later, we tried to do the same thing to a girl that was a lot younger, in a treehouse we hung out in. You never know how things are going to affect you. I'm sure the stuff that I'm talking about has much to do with who I became and my values and my morals regarding women and other things.

The next year we moved to New Maryland. My dad worked for a lumber mill. We lived in a little 10 foot by 10 foot shack, on the property. It was made out of rough lumber and the cracks were so large you could see through them. All of our furniture was made of rough lumber as well. There was a kitchen and one bedroom. I remember on cold nights, mom would heat the old cast irons, wrap them in newspaper, and put them at the bottom of our beds to keep our feet warm. In the morning my father would have to break the ice in the water pail so we could wash.

At the age of eight I had to walk three miles to school and back each day. I was back in a one-room school again. I was still wearing old, used clothes and this poverty separated me from the others, and I grew up thinking I was bad.

There are good things I remember about my father. He always had time for me. He read to me every night until I could read for myself. He played checkers with me and taught me other games. Although we were extremely poor, my parents always showed me attention. Even though my mother was verbally and physically abusive, I knew she loved me in her own way.

We moved back to Hanwell's Settlement and for the next five years, I was back in the one-room school there. I had a female cousin who went there too. She was a day older than me. She always held that over me. One day we were fighting and she said "well at least I'm not adopted". I just remember that ringing in my ears. It reverberated through my mind. Adopted, I thought "adopted ... who's adopted?".

I discovered at the age of eight or nine that I was adopted. That changed my life. I was no longer the same as all the other children. They all had real moms and dads and knew who they were.

Hanwell Settlement was this long hill. There were farms and houses on both sides. There were about 27 families at the Settlement then. I tried to imagine, as I walked past the houses, what it would be like to live there. What would it be like to be in a real family, where you had a real mom and dad. I felt like I came from outer space or something. I felt totally ostracized and isolated. I didn't know then what effect it was going to have on me later in life.

I was sexually assaulted and abused various times by a church member in Hanwell Settlement. (He also abused his younger brother who I used to play with). Most of the abuse went on in their farmhouse, but sometimes he would be out preying and looking for kids along the road. The odd time he'd catch me on a lonely stretch of road. He was a big guy probably weighed a couple of hundred pounds. This man raped me by dragging me into the woods one day and having his way with me. I felt ashamed, degraded and full of guilt.

45

In December, 1956, a few months past my tenth birthday, my father got pneumonia. My mother wanted him to go to the hospital but he didn't want to because it was close to Christmas. One day I was sitting in class and I watched the ambulance take my dad away. I had all these questions. I was only ten. I wondered where were they taking my dad. What's wrong? What are they going to do with him? How serious is the situation? Little did I know that would be the last time I would see my father alive.

I remember Mom sending me to stay at the neighbours, Clifford and Myrtle who lived next door to my Uncle Fred. Mom went into the Victoria Public Hospital in Fredericton to visit my dad. Things were worse than they thought. Mom decided she needed to stay the night at the hospital. I remember after I was in bed, Edna Shaw, my aunt came to the door and was whispering that my dad had passed away. My mother was in town making funeral arrangements. I remember laying in bed trying to sleep. It was like a nightmare... what had they done with my dad? I didn't want to accept the fact that it was true.

I remember the later years of my dad's life ... how he read to me; played checkers with me, and even the night before the ambulance took him, he sat up and read with me. My father was like that. He'd take me for walks in the woods and show me different kinds of trees. It seemed I had a closer relationship with my father than with my mother, although I didn't know why. That night all those things were going through my head. I just thought that if I fell asleep, when I woke up, it would all be over. My mother would be there, my father would be there, everything would be fine. He'd get out of the hospital and life would go on. It never happened.

A few days later my dad was buried in the Presbyterian Church in Hanwell Settlement. I remember going to the funeral that day and all the sadness, hurt and pain that was in my heart as I watched them lower my father into the ground. A legion member came from town and played The Last Post on the bugle. It was December the 18th, 1956, a week before Christmas. I was crying. My mother pulled me aside and told me not to cry. She said that I was the man of the house now and I had to look after her. Well I was only 10 years old and I really didn't feel like being the man of the house. I just felt like a lost, hurt little boy, living some kind of grotesque nightmare, and hoping I'd wake up and it would all go away. It didn't. Over time you forget and the grieving goes away. But I know now that there were things in my heart that would be there for the next 35 years.

By the age of ten, I was doomed for failure. There was a lot of physical and verbal abuse from my mom. I didn't understand why my mother would beat me, sometimes for no reason at all. I remember having child welfare at our house when I was about seven. They wanted to take me away from her. My mother and father had told me what to say if these people came and wanted to take me. I said all the right things . When it comes right down to it, whether they beat me harder than they should have or not, they were my parents and I didn't want to be taken away from them. The verbal and physical abuse from my mom, the sexual abuse outside the home, the feelings of abandonment after my dad's death would all affect my future dramatically.

After my father died, mom would take me to Uncle Rolly's where I'd work on the farm whenever I could. For the next couple of years at Easter, Christmas and summer vacation, I'd work there. The trouble working for Rolly was, that he never had time for kids. He gave you a man's work and expected you to do it. Although I liked him and my Aunt, I remember the tyranny of working on the farm. I'd get up at 5:30 a.m., go to the barn, milk a dozen cows, separate the milk and feed the cows. I'd come in at 7:30 or 8:00 for breakfast then back out till dinner. In the wintertime I'd have to lug water. My little bean pole arms filled 45 gallon drums. I carried five gallon bucket's one in each arm. There was no time for play. Looking back now, I understand that he was a man. He didn't want to play. What he didn't understand was that I was a boy and I needed to play. I needed time to have new friends. I needed time to adapt to life without a dad.

Many times my Aunt Elva would give me candy and different things to help me through those times. When I was about 12, I biked from Hanwell to Rolly's to work on the farm. I had some friends and in July and August they'd want to take off swimming. That wasn't good enough for him. One day he just kicked my butt and told me to get off the farm. He didn't want me any more. I got on my bike, sort of heartbroken, heading for Hanwell... heading for home. From these experiences I learned not to have a high value for working because I never got paid and was never good enough.

After my dad died, my mother had a hard time with me. I continued to go to church with her for a couple of years but lost interest because I blamed God for my father's death. I didn't feel like serving a God who couldn't save a kid's father. I had no further need of Him.

I ended up going to Junior High at Albert Street School in Fredericton, NB. I was an avid reader and always made good marks. I remember when I was eight years old, I read a book a day. The poverty mentality and the various abuses inside and outside the home, continued into my teen years. As a result, I lost interest in school. I had no value for sports and eventually started to hang out at Roy's Pool Room. I'd go down there at noon and come back in time to catch the bus home. The only thing that was good about my teenage days was that I learned to shoot pool.

Two trips through Grade 9. I'd had enough! I quit school and decided to go out to work. One of the first jobs I got was delivering messages for the CPR or CNR. Back then they had no computers and no e-mail. I was a messenger boy and delivered messages around town on my bicycle. I did that for two or three weeks. They paid me about $18 a week. My friend worked at the Hartt Shoe Factory for $55 a week, about three times the money I made. So at 16 I got a job at the Hartt Shoe Factory. I used to travel back and forth to work with the people who worked in the mill. I had a hankering to find out more about city life. I was no longer interested in staying in Hanwell Settlement.

I found myself a place on King Street. It was a boarding house and I began to stay there and hang around Fredericton. In those days there were a couple of dance halls, the IOF Hall and the KP Hall downtown on Carlton Street. I was hanging out down there with two brothers, Jim and Jerry Tripp. A lot of us hung around Bill's Snack Bar, a little restaurant down on Carlton Street.

I found that there was quite a few people who didn't work. They quit school like I did. They were five or six years older than me and some had already been in jail. I started hanging with them and we did a lot of illegal things together, like breaking and entering, shoplifting and such, mostly to buy booze. More than anything, I wanted to fit in and drinking helped me do that. I remember the first time I drank alcohol. I got deathly sick on a six pack of beer. I swore I'd never drink it again. But there was something about it that I enjoyed. It wasn't the sickness or the hangover, but it seemed to make me feel good. I'd gone through a lot in my life not feeling good. I realized that if you got drunk and passed out you felt good. So I began to drink. I didn't know in my early teens that drinking alcohol was going to make me a teenage alcoholic.

I worked in the shoe factory for about three and a half years. I worked a couple of years and got fired. I jigged around for the summer and came back and got a job there again and worked for a couple of years more. I drank more and more. The only reason I lasted so long was that most of the people who worked there were also heavy drinkers. It was this common ground that kept me there.

I was a good worker and I remember working in the making department, I could run 18 out of the 24 machines. So I was sort of an in-between. Every time someone was out, they'd put me on their machine. I learned a lot about making a shoe, but they never paid me the right money. Guys on some of the machines that I was running back then were making $80 - $100 a day, and I was working for about $55 bucks a week. Even though I had a steady job, I still hung out on the streets with the guys, partying and living it up.

After a while, my work weeks became two-day work weeks and five-day weekends, so I wasn't much value to them. I wanted to quit and they wanted me out, so I made them fire me. I collected my pay and walked out the door. I drew unemployment for a while. I stayed drunk all that summer. I got involved in hanging around in Marysville, another place on the north side of Fredericton. Marysville was built by a man named Boss Gibson. He built a cotton mill there in the 1800's and here it was in the 1960's.

There was a group of guys there called the "Wild String". They'd work hard all week in the cotton mill, then head to the Boisetown dance on Saturday night. They'd be very drunk and looking for a fight. Hanging out with these guys, I really learned to fight. It was the next thing to living on the street, although we all had homes, boarding houses or places where we stayed. I learned to drink real well, fight real well and our escapades took us to Minto, Lakeville Corner, Stanley and Boisetown, all within an hour's drive of Marysville. We'd go looking for women and for trouble. I hung with the "Wild String". There was me, Rusty, Bill and others. We'd drop over to these places and fight with anybody. We were so bad that nobody wanted anything to do with us. No-one invited us to their parties. We'd just go there and raise hell.

I remember working in the mill when I fell in love for the first time. I was about 21 or 22 years old. This girl came from an upper middle-class family. They were well known in the Town of Marysville. I hooked up with her for two or three years. The relationship became sexual and she got pregnant. I was an alcoholic; full of confusion and fear. I remember going to town, in her father's car, to pick up a marriage license. I was freaking. I had no idea how I was going to support her. I had a hard time supporting my alcohol addiction. I finally said, "I don't think I can marry you, you'd better take me home. For the next eight to ten years, I tried to drink myself to death. It wasn't that I didn't love her, but I couldn't see how fair it was to her, being married to me.

I couldn't imagine how to help her keep or raise that child. I thought she would be better off on her own. We split company that day and other than a rendezvous later, we never really spoke for the next 22 years. Life without Christ is filled with mistakes and hardships and this was one of them. She had a son.

I had nothing left to live for, and didn't care about anything. I began to drink really hard. There was a place up in the back of Marysville where I was living called Millbrook. In the 1800's they had built a dam there. We swam and hung out there. This was during the Hippie Movement. This is when I started getting involved in other things during the early 70's.

One night I got drunk and did LSD, a drug I was dead against. I remember coming down after about 12 hours of hallucinations. The only thing I could think of the next day was that my opinion about drugs had changed . I moved out of the boarding house and spent a summer living in the woods, living in a tent, living wherever liquor and drugs took me.

I became a wino during the Hippie Movement. I had no money. I just lived from hand to mouth. I spent the next several years of my life being a wino, living on the streets, panhandling, stealing or whatever I had to do. I was on a downward spiral. Although I got involved with drugs, alcohol was still my drug of choice. I lived in a tavern six days a week, except in the summertime when I lived at Millbrook. I remember many of the guys back then, we were all searching for something and we tried to find it anywhere we could.

The next thing I knew I was 29. I never had much involvement with women in those few years. I was just too drunk all the time; too full of hurt and pain, broken hearts, broken dreams, broken promises and broken realities. I didn't want anything to do with anybody. I didn't care whether I lived or died. There were different girls along the way but nothing substantial. Then I met Kathy and she began to live with me.

That summer, 1985, I ended up in the hospital in Intensive Care. During those last couple of years of alcoholism, I remember thinking that anybody who bought food was crazy. I thought it was a total waste of money. I spent my money totally on booze and I ate a couple of meals a week. When you run your body that hard, on alcohol, beer and wine, you don't take any money for food. If you don't nourish your body, it's just a matter of time before it breaks down and mine did.

I had pancreatitis. I was home alone in the basement apartment where I lived with Kathy. She was in town working. I was deathly sick. I phoned a friend of mine, Mark, who came and picked me up. I thank God he was home that day. If he hadn't been, I would have died.

I layed in that hospital room going in and out of consciousness. My temperature was around 112. The doctor walked out of the room because he didn't know what was wrong. An elderly doctor came into the room and realized I had pancreatitis. Then he got me into Emergency. I remember he came in the next day. I asked him "How bad is it?" He asked me, "Do you really wanted to know". I replied, "If I didn't want to know, I wouldn't have asked". He said, "Well son you got an 80% chance of dying". You know it's funny because for the last eight or ten years I didn't care whether I lived or died but now, there seemed to be something in me that didn't want to die. I had one chance in five of making it. I believe now, if I hadn't focused all my energy and effort into trying to live, I would have died. Even then, God was involved in my life although I wasn't involved with Him.

Not only did I almost die that day, but I almost died four times while I was in Intensive Care during the next four months. I went through different operations. They cut me from side to side. They had tubes in me everywhere. I lost 55 lbs in two or three weeks at the beginning of that ordeal. I couldn't even drink water. I had to rinse my mouth and put an ice cube in it. I had bedsores all over me and my hips were black and blue from the needles that gave me morphine. My veins all shrunk up from the intravenous that was trying to keep me alive. I was admitted in July and left in October.

I spent months recuperating. One time during the process, they told me if I could walk down a set of stairs I could leave. I didn't realize that after being bedridden for a couple of months the muscles in your legs weaken. I got up, walked down a set of stairs and back up. I pulled all the muscles in the back of my legs. For that little trick, I walked on crutches for a couple of months, then began using a cane. I guess it took about a year to recuperate. Kathy sat beside my bed and walked with me through that whole ordeal. She was a great support. The pressure on her must have been tremendous. She was my encouragement and hope. I realized during this time that I should never drink alcohol again. I was told this by all the specialists.

I believe Jesus met me in the hospital. I'll share a story that comes to mind that I heard many years later when I was sharing my life story at a young offenders facility. After I finished a nurse in the facility came over and said, "Can I tell another part of that story of your life?"

She tells the story about working an afternoon shift in Intensive Care in Victoria Public Hospital several years before. It was the same time I was in that hospital. There was a major traffic accident in Gary about 15 miles outside Fredericton. There were people hurt and they needed a bed in Intensive Care. They made a decision to put me on a gurney in the hallway to die and make room for the accident victim.

To this day I've no idea what that decision was based on. I think a couple of things. I was just a streeter, a long haired, alcoholic hippie of no particular value to anyone. I'd almost died three or four times in there and they didn't expect me to live anyway. They had to make a choice and I was it. From the time they got the call from the ambulance, they were making arrangements to put the accident victim in the Intensive Care Unit.

An elderly man beside me had a cardiac arrest and died. She said, "I could never understand why a rotten person like you had to live and that nice old man had to die". She said, "I never understood it until today, when I saw you standing before me in this young offenders facility sharing Jesus Christ". Then that whole thing came back to her and it began to make sense for the first time.

I'd never heard about that part of my life before. It showed me, that Jesus was very much involved in my life. He had a purpose for me even then. I didn't understand that then. Paul said in Romans 5:8 "while we were yet sinners (and believe me I was a sinner and like Paul I was the chief of sinners) Christ died for us". I just thank God for His grace and His mercy.

I did survive and got back up and running. I began to smoke a little pot. There was a dry spell in Fredericton. That means there were no drugs around. I knew these hippie guys who lived in a co-op down in Devon and they had some.

I remember talking to Kathy, and saying "look we got a welfare cheque on Thursday. I don't have to pay the landlord till Monday, why don't I take this cheque and invest it in a pound of pot?". Back then you could buy a pound of Mexican for about $135 - $185 depending on who you were and where you bought it. I'll buy a pound of pot, break it up, sell a few bags and get our money back. We'll have a couple of bags to smoke ourselves. That was enough for my addiction. I told her the worst case scenario was that I'd get busted and go to prison for four to six months. We made the decision to do it. She was involved, not in the dealing but in the essence of it. It was okay with her.

I bought a pound of pot, came home and cut it up and sold it in four hours. I was inspired to say the least. I went back and bought two pounds, came home, cut them up and sold them in about a day. Went back down and bought four pounds, cut them up and sold them all. By Monday morning I had sold seven pounds of pot. I had my money ready for the rent. I had some bags of pot to smoke. I had some money in my pocket and I even bought an old American Buick for about $150. Things had changed in three or four days in my life. I remember when we moved into that place all we had was a baby mattress that someone had left behind. I had made a major investment and won.

A new idea entered my life, drug dealing. Maybe I'll just sell a few pounds, make a little money, get nice furniture, then we'll just quit and I'll be able to support my habit. I'd been poor all my life, never had anything, never had a new bike or anything. I just thought it would be nice to have a few dollars to survive; get a nice, little place in the country, nothing too expensive, sort of a Cinderella story. It would read "lived happily ever after".

I didn't know where that journey was going to take me. The same as we have no idea where any journey's gonna take us in life. It's like I said, the first joint of marijuana you smoke, the first pin puff of hash,. the first pill you drop, the first needle you put in your arm, the first alcohol you drink ... you've made that conscious decision. But no-one ever decides when they're going to make it their last one. Many people end up in prison. Many end up dead. Many end up addicted. They have broken homes, broken lives and broken dreams, all because of alcohol and drugs. My life reeked of all that.

So I'm on the rebound now. I'm 30 years old. I'm dealing drugs and the next thing you know I'm making $500 or $600 out my front door. For the first time in my life, I have real money. It's quite a thing for a poor kid that isn't highly educated, doesn't have any contacts for good jobs, doesn't have a trade, and he's making $500 or $600 a week. My lifestyle began to change. I always had money in my pocket and drugs to smoke. I had an old car to drive that gave me a sense of identity. I was someone, a drug dealer. People would want to hook up with me to buy a bag of pot or a dime bag or a nickel. Back then, there were a lot of nickel and dime bags. I was one of many guys who was doing this back in my town.

That year many people got involved. Some lasted as long as I did and some didn't. Some didn't manage their business right and just smoked what they got. I had kind of a vision back then. I wanted a house, a car, some furniture and then I'd quit. I'd get a real job. I'd settle down and I'd work the rest of my life. That was my thinking. Little did I know that there was much more to it than that. Not only did I get hooked on marijuana, and later on hash and many other drugs, I got hooked on money. I didn't place as great a value on money as my friends did. I was hooked in that lifestyle. I could go out and eat whenever I wanted and I could buy whatever I wanted. So wheeling and dealing became a way of life.

Over the next year or so, I was selling 10 lbs. a week. I made connections stateside and elsewhere. People would bring me 10 lbs. every week. I'd bag it up in 160 or 180 bags and I'd put it out my front door in Marysville. Money was coming in so fast, I couldn't spend it. The more dope I had, the more I smoked. I turned everybody else on. I turned all kinds of friends on and I was free with my dope.

Millbrook was still a party spot. Friday and Saturday nights, some nights through the week, sometimes every week. When I wasn't home dealing, I was hanging out there, smoking my pot. I was impressing people and being impressed by people. I remember one summer, I went to Millbrook every night. I'd take a couple of bags of pot and I'd sit down somewhere and I'd roll up the whole two bags. Then we'd smoke them. It was the same every night. I was turning people on. People were coming to listen to me talk about everything from God to drugs. I could never get this God thing out of my mind. I told people I'm going to have a new four wheel drive and they thought I was out of my mind. They told me I was crazy. I told them, "You watch and see". I'd gotten on to what I thought was a good thing. I knew when opportunity knocked. I felt like I'd just discovered Amway, and I was the first one in.

Things became good for me. No more poverty! No more wondering where I was going to get my next meal. I got a nice car and good clothes. I was still into the hippie scene, so it was new jeans or new shirts or whatever. I also enjoyed sharing my drugs with all my friends. My place was always party time. Dope was free.

I'd made some good connections. I wanted to sell pounds so I got people who had bought bags under me to sell bags. I got a friend to take over my business doing all the bagging. I moved my business from my house to Millbrook. He didn't know how that was gonna happen. So I said, "You just sit on this rock like I do, and when people come, you give them bags, like I'm giving them bags". He made all kinds of money that summer and ended up getting busted and going to jail.

I kept on dealing ... making money ... selling dope ...smoking dope ... partying .... making money. Every day was the same. I became really good at hiding dope, and stashing dope. I never kept dope in my house. I got real street smart. I began buying scanners. I taught all the people that worked for me how to use them. I had a mobile scanner in my truck and one in my home. I tuned in to the police and always knew what they were doing. I advised all the guys that worked with me to do the same.

You couldn't buy scanners in Fredericton. We had to go down to Bangor in the States and buy Bearcat Scanners. I had connections in the States and in Ontario. My business got bigger and bigger. I had more and more people working for me.

I was selling 30 to 50 lbs a week and worked 80 to 100 hours a week. I worked hard. I cut trails through the woods for skidoos in the wintertime . I cut trails in the summer time for three-wheelers and four-wheelers. I moved around the city. I never stayed in one place for too long. I could always move my business. I wanted to build my business bigger and better than any one else in my area, and I wanted to make money. I also wanted to stay out of prison and did for a long time.

In the late 70's or early 80's I got busted because of a friend of my mine who was talking on the phone. I ended up in court on two conspiracy charges, trafficking in marijuana and hashish with two other guys. I got busted five times for conspiracy, the fifth time was in 1982. I hired a lawyer and paid him big bucks. I went to court but I won the case the first four times I was busted. I knew that you had to spend money to have a good lawyer. The police had bugged my phone for about 12 years. That's the lifestyle I was in. I was busted four times and beat the charges each time.

In 1982, I was in a motorcycle accident. A redneck cut me off in a gravel truck because I was a known drug dealer. I believe he tried to kill me. I had to take to the ditch and ended up with two pins in my leg. I broke my knee in six places. My bike was banged up a bit and my friend was knocked off the back. While I was in the hospital, the police broke into my house, bugged my phone and were setting me up for when I got out.

At this time I lived in Harvey, about 35 miles out of Fredericton towards the main St. Stephen/McAdam border. I moved up there because it was close to the border and I did a lot of dealing with people in the States. I also did a lot of dealing with some very influential people in the Montreal area. I was dealing day and night. I was always busy and I made all kinds of money. At this time I had worked up to a two or three million dollar a year business. I had about 35 people working for me and they in turn had dozens of foot soldiers under them. We had a successful business. I lived in a nice house. I had three-wheelers and four-wheelers, leather jackets for every day of the week. I really had a poverty mentality so I had all kinds of clothes. I had a brand new pool table. I had everything I wanted, nice car, skidoos, guns, everything.

Yet I was always looking for something else. I didn't know what it was but I was looking for something else. That's where I was at this point in my life.

We were busted with a conspiracy to traffic in cocaine. My partner, Ben and my girlfriend Karen (who's now my wife), had been busted at the Milltown border. They didn't follow instructions and they were caught with an ounce of cocaine. Karen had it hidden on her. They charged them with conspiracy to traffic cocaine into Canada. They kept Karen and Benny in jail overnight. The next morning, they raided my house. I was in Fredericton. They arrested Kathy, my live-in girlfriend at the time. When I phoned from Fredericton, she told me the police were there. I went and turned myself in. We were all in the Brunswick Street Jail waiting to go up for bail hearing.

During the month in Brunswick Street, I began to read my Bible. I'd been involved in a cocaine addiction then for about four or five years. We were stoned all through court right up until the actual sentencing. I'd had no break from cocaine or any of the drugs. I remember coming down hard and had trouble sleeping the first couple of weeks. I managed to beat the addiction. In the midst of all that I thought about Jesus and my Christian upbringing. I guess it was the first time in a long time that I had taken any stock of my life. It's funny how your thoughts will turn to Jesus when you are in a bind. The reality is, He's always there. The Bible says, "He'll never leave us or forsake us". It is we who leave and forsake Him.

I remember sitting on my top bunk about three o'clock in the morning. There were about half a dozen of us in the cell, and it was there that I made a commitment to Jesus Christ. It was just a verbal commitment out of my own mouth and heart. I began to read the Bible for the next couple of weeks. I used to get static from the others for reading my Bible, but I was sitting on my bunk reading it to myself. I never read it out loud so there'd be no confrontations. I was an old streeter who knew how to fight. "You guys play your cards or watch your t.v., just leave me alone, all I'm doing is reading this Bible to myself", was my response.

They had a hearing and we put up $5,000 or $10,000 bail and they let us out and we went about our business. We went to court and the conspiracy to traffic cocaine was thrown out on a technicality. They analyzed it and found it was cocaine with something else in it so we beat that charge. We were found guilty of conspiracy to traffic hashish into Canada. This was ironic because the hashish they were talking about was an ounce with a street value of about $250.00. You could imagine four people going to the States to buy this ounce of hash. There was obviously no conspiracy. Nevertheless we were sentenced. I got two years in the federal penitentiary in Dorchester for this first offense. My girlfriend got six months, Karen got three months and Ben got six months.

I ended up going to Dorchester which was maximum security in those days. I was only there a couple of weeks but I was locked up 23 1/2 hours a day and got a half an hour out in the yard. I remember trying to watch T.V. There was one for about every three cells. You had to get your head between the bars to watch it. It was a lot of hassle. I had decided that if I ever did get sent to prison, I wanted to read the Bible. I took a month and I read it from cover to cover.

I was never away from the Bible. When I lived in Harvey and was having cocaine parties, I'd have a select number of friends over and we'd do three or four thousand dollars worth of drugs overnight. I would always read the Bible. I'll admit my reasons probably weren't good. I believed in God, Heaven and Hell and the Devil. I knew one thing, although I didn't want to be a Christian, I still didn't want to go to Hell. I thought if I interpreted the prophesies of the Old Testament and found out when Jesus was coming, I'd at least get my foot in the door, and wouldn't end up in Hell. Unfortunately, that wasn't a good reason to be reading it, but nevertheless I believe the Lord used that time to get His Word in my heart.

One Sunday morning after a night of doing acid with some friends. We came home to clean up and then hit the road again. My house was just that, a house, it was never a home. My friend Rusty and I were in the process of getting cleaned up. He was watching t.v. as I showered and then it was his turn in the shower. While I was waiting for Rusty I watched t.v. as well. Jimmy Swaggert was on. I began to watch the sermon and the Holy Spirit convicted me and I wept. When Rusty came out of the shower, I straightened up my act because I was too macho to show my true emotions.

About ten years later, Rusty and I had both become Christians and one day I shared that incident with him. He looked at me and laughed. Apparently the same thing had happened to him when I was in the shower. It's amazing that even during those times, Jesus was calling out to me even though I was out of my mind on drugs. He had a purpose and plan for me even then.

Next I was transferred to Springhill which was a medium security institution. I began studying the Bible for the next four and a half months that I was there. I spent a little over six months on a two year sentence in a Federal penitentiary and I got out on appeal bail. I've still got that old NIV brown, hard cover Bible. I spent many times especially Saturdays and Sundays, sitting in my cell reading the Word. I was involved in the Chapel services. I was bold about the Lord. I shared Him with different people in the prison, and I was challenged for my Christianity. Some people thought it was just a ploy to get out, but it was real. I believed I was real. I believed I was a Christian. I wanted to be a Christian and I wanted to make it. I believe many people today are doing the same thing.

I vowed in my heart if I ever went to prison, I would not look back on it as a negative experience. I read the Bible cover to cover. It's the first time, except as a child, that I made a serious commitment to Jesus Christ. I learned a lot about the Lord through studying the bible. I got my GED. I got my certificate for Grade 12 education and I took a course on small gas engines in the shop. I worked out on the weights six days a week. I got in really good shape. I met a variety of people from all over Canada and the States. I learned a lot about offenders. A lot of the stuff I learned then, I'm applying today. So I can't really say, that it was a bad time in my life. It was the first time in a long time, where God had gotten me in a place where He could talk to me, and I was in a place I would listen.

I had a visit from my girlfriend, Karen who is now my wife. I went to the visiting room and I walked by her. She'd weighed about 88 lbs. when she went to jail and I weighed about 150 lbs. I'd beefed up about 25 lbs and she had put on about 20 lbs. In the midst of cocaine, drugs and partying, we had become very unhealthy and didn't even realize it. I walked by her. We didn't recognize each other. I sat down with some other friends that had come to visit. After about 10 minutes they said, "Aren't you going to visit with your girlfriend?" I realized that it was Karen there to visit me.

I remember the income tax people and others trying to get a hold of me to tell me I owed them money. They were sending me letters in Dorchester and in Springhill. They wanted money and I didn't have any. Although at this point I had managed millions of dollars. I squandered that money on drug abuse, mostly on cocaine . It didn't have any value to me. There's an old saying "easy come, easy go", and in some sense I guess that's true.

One of the things I learned from prison, is that prison doesn't make people good . Prison doesn't make you change your mind or your heart. Prison is not a place where people get out and say, "Well, I'm not gonna go there again". Prison itself cannot deter anyone from a life of crime. I think most times, prison makes you bitter and angry. Most people are arrested for making bad decisions. In other words, you are irresponsible. You can't make good decisions. Then you're incarcerated in a place where you don't have an opportunity to make any decisions. You don't have to colour code your socks or your t-shirt, your pants or your coat, it's all done for you. You don't have to turn the lights on or off, or open any doors, it's all done for you. You don't have to worry about supper, what you're having or where your having it, it's all done for you. So if you take a bunch of people who can't make good decisions, put them in a place where they don't have a chance to exercise their decision making process, then let them back out into the community, where they have to make decisions, they'll still make poor ones. The reality is that most will re-offend and go back to jail. Prison doesn't work. They need Jesus. "Whom the Son sets free is free indeed" (John 8:36).

Although I was a Christian through the whole thing, it put bitterness in my heart. I was not guilty of the charges that I was sent to prison for. I was guilty of probably tens of thousands of other ones, but the actual charges that I was sent to prison for, I never committed. That sentencing process only refueled any negativity I had in my heart. The neat thing about it all was that not only did I learn all that stuff, but I stood on my faith throughout the whole thing.

It is sad to say sometimes you have to be incarcerated or be down and out to get up. Many times that is what we do have to do in life. We have to be on the bottom before we start reaching out. Jesus didn't make these things happen in my life. He allowed me to come to a place where I had to draw strength from outside myself. Only then, could He get my attention. I thought like a lot of people about religion or that Christian thing. That's for weak people! I didn't think I was a weak person. I had masterminded an organization. I had masses of people working for me. I was very successful at what I did, so I knew I had the capability of being a survivor and a leader.

I got out of jail on appeal bail at a bit over six months. When I went to jail I had several girlfriends and I still have a box full of letters that we exchanged. I was convicted in prison and I knew I had to be a man of one woman. I made a decision to pick Karen. There was Cindy, Karen and another girl. Karen and I had a daughter named Jennifer who was a little over a year old. Cindy and I had a daughter named Natasha, a year and a half old. The other girl had no children by me. It was a hard decision, but I knew I had to make it. Although I kept in contact with these women while I was in prison, when I got out I chose to live with Karen. I took her for my girlfriend and I hoped it would progress to where she would be my wife.

While I was in Springhill Institution there were five suicides, that summer in the Atlantic Region, my friend Gary Shields was one of them.

When I was first released to the street, I moved back into my house in Traceyville and began to attend a little Pentecostal Church in Beaver Dam. I had never been in a church where there had been teaching about dealing with your own hurt or pain, shame, guilt, rejection, unworthiness or low self-esteem. It was just go to church on Sunday, mid-week service, read your Bible and that was basically it. So although I was a Christian and was saved, I didn't know how to deal with any of that stuff inside me.

The sad reality was that when I was released from prison, I was still bound by my own hurts and burdens and I needed a massive amount of healing. I was in a mental prison of my own making. I never had any way to escape from the sexual, verbal, and physical abuse, plus all the trappings that I had added to it with drugs, alcohol, violence, crime and rages. I didn't know if there was a way to deal with it or escape from it. There never was the peace or the joy that I really needed. I feel that many people today are like I was and they don't know what to do about it either.

I lived the Christian lifestyle for about eight months. If you are reading this and you can't relate to this, neither could we. We didn't get up one day and say this church stuff isn't for us. We didn't get offended in the church or anything like that. It was a very subtle thing. I believe the enemy, Satan, is very subtle in how he does things. He undermined us in our own relationship and in our relationship with the Lord. Things like watching the late show on a Saturday night, you wake up the next morning and you're too tired to go to church. You think maybe we'll go tonight instead. Night would roll around and you say maybe we'll go next week. Little things cause a sliding away.

Another problem was finances. We were used to having all kinds of money and now we were financially strapped. My concern for offenders is that we give them all kinds of programs and stuff, but we don't give them the one thing they need, and that's a job. Most of the people I've worked with over the last ten or twelve years needed a job when they got out of prison.

I was like that. I didn't have a job or any education so I ended up on welfare. I lived in Tracy which was 20 minutes from town. I would have to decide what day of the week I was going to town so I could do everything on that day. Once I got home, I couldn't go anywhere for another week. My house became a prison.

I was starving for fellowship as well. I would go to church, arrive just before service began and sit in the back row. Then I was the first one out the door so I didn't talk to anyone. Desperate for companionship, I started hanging out with an old friend who was a druggie. He would go to bed about 4 a.m. and get up at about 2 p.m, so I knew his schedule. I could pop by when I had gas money to hang out. He'd play electric guitar and smoke a few joints and I thought that was cool.

I was a Christian then and didn't do dope. Who knows, I might even be able to witness to him. That was my thinking. I'd win him to the Lord. Little did I know that was part of Satan's plan to undermine me, and draw me back to my old lifestyle. I never anticipated that. Satan has a plan for everybody. We are told that Jesus has a plan for our life which is true, but rarely are we warned that Satan has a plan for us too.

One day when I was really bummed out and discouraged, I went to visit my buddy. I got to thinking "gee, I'll just have a few puffs off the joint he was smoking and that would be good. I could just chill out, mellow out, just relax and take the pressure off". I was stressed to the max because of my finances and other things. The next thing I knew, I was asking him for a puff. He argued with me because he knew I was a Christian. I convinced him to let me have some and I smoked a third of a joint. I went home, hid that from my wife, had supper and went to bed.

The next day I was back there, I got stoned again and the day after that. I used money, that was supposed to be for groceries and bills for gas so I could get there and get stoned. The next thing I knew, I had him roll up some big joints. I told him I would take them home and roll up some little pin joints. The old saying misery loves company is true. I began to turn my wife on. We'd put the baby to bed after supper and we'd smoke the little pin joints and watch tv. We were amazed that we could smoke so little and get high. That only lasted for a day or two. Then we would have to smoke a whole joint to get high. One thing led to another and this led to us getting stoned not only in the evening but during the day as well.

The next thing I knew I just wasn't bumming joints, I was getting a quarter bag here and a half bag there. I still had all these connections from my past. It was easy for me to go to them because they knew and trusted me and I could get fronts. At the end of the next month, I was really in an economic bind. I owed money for dope I couldn't pay. The only thing I kept during all the drug and alcohol days was my word. I talked to some people and told them that I was interested in selling some small lots of dope.

Here I was on appeal bail for $5,000, having to sign in once or twice a week, and I was running pot across the Province. I thought, "I'll just do a few deals to get back on my feet, catch up on my bills, buy some groceries and get some extra money for gas, and then I'll quit". It was good thinking, but it didn't end up that way. I got back into the drugs, drinking and smoking heavier. It was nice to have money again. I was back into the whole scene again. Satan had a plan and I fell for it thinking all the time that I knew what I was doing.

I look back on that time now and I remember what the Bible says about keeping your house in order. If you don't keep your house in order, the spirit that was driven out will come back, bring seven other spirits with it and you will be worse off than before. I lived that whole parable. In the next six or eight months that spirit came back and brought seven more with it. It was worse than ever before. (Matthew 12: 43-45)

A couple of years of dealing and building my business and I was making $6,000 - $7,000 a week. I was able to afford all the toys. I was building my empire back up. One night, we were getting ready to go to a biker club house. I heard about some good cocaine in town that had just come from Florida. I told my wife that I knew the damage cocaine could do and swore I would never do it again. I had experienced the addiction to it and knew what it was about, so I'd just buy a couple of grams. We'll do them and that will be it.

We bought a couple of grams of cocaine and that was the beginning of another four and half to five year nightmare. I built my business back into $250,000 to $300,000 per year. I had it all back and yet it wasn't the same.

I know now that once a person is serious about committing their heart to Jesus Christ, you can backslide but it will never be the same again. I couldn't forget Jesus. I was always reminded of Him. I couldn't shake it no matter how stoned I got. I wasn't serving Him and that haunted me for the next five or six years. My life became much worse. Karen also became addicted to cocaine. I was selling massive amounts of dope to pay for our addiction. She was doing coke behind my back. I would come home and she would steal money from me and get people to bring her cocaine. We had all kinds of people in our house at any given time of the day. The women in the community would be here because there would always be free dope.

Although we lived under the same roof, we lived separate lifestyles. Somewhere through the process, I decided I should marry my wife. Karen's parents didn't want her to marry me as they were Christians and she was a backslidden Christian. I used to think that if we got married, they would be happy. We got married in a Pentecostal Church, had the reception in a Wesleyan Church and the party in a Catholic Church. We didn't want to be biased so we utilized three different denominations to go through the process. A lot of her Christian friends from her Mother's side came to the wedding at the church and some of our friends. On one side of the church were the Christians and on the other side were the gangsters and dealers. None of the Christians went to the party that night because it was totally drugs and alcohol, just crazy stuff.

65

At the time we got married, Karen was pregnant with our second child, Meaghan. We were still hooked in the old lifestyle. I was still wheeling and dealing. There were all kinds of parties going on. I beat her up lots of times. She was stealing my money and we'd get into fights over it. She'd blame someone else or say she didn't know where the money went. She'd justify it somehow. I was running around on her with different women from the biker clubhouse and other places. I knew one thing, she had stolen $100,000 to $200,000 dollars over a period of two or three years. She wasn't the woman I met. And I wasn't the man she met. We had become two totally different people. That's what drugs and addiction will do to you.

Our marriage was falling apart. Although we saw it happening, we didn't talk about it as our communication lines were down. We were in complete denial. We were living under the same roof, having children and having sex. In a crazy way, we loved each other.

There was a lot of violence and stealing. I'd put money together to pay off the people I worked with. They'd come back to see me as the payments were short and I couldn't figure that out. She would be fingering the money, just a hundred dollars out of different piles. This put my life in jeopardy. They'd come back and confront me about it and I'd have to dig up the money to pay them. Karen ended up in a transition house at one point in St. John with all the kids. She wouldn't go to one in Fredericton. I was a violent aggressor. The police were scared of me. My wife was scared of me and so were a lot of my friends. Somewhere in the insanity of my own mind, I knew that this was not really me.

The police continued to harass me on a daily basis. My phones were tapped again. Once I got stopped three times in half an hour. There were many incidents of violence in this lifestyle. I learned how to defend myself because I knew that the police would never help me because I was a convicted drug dealer.

In 1989, Karen was eight and a half months pregnant with my fourth daughter (after Meaghan, there was Samantha Jo) and we decided to go to see the Rolling Stones in Toronto. We rented a van. We had Natasha with us (my daughter from my relationship with Cindy). Cindy and her boyfriend were

66

living common-law in Toronto. We were taking Natasha back home. My son, who was 19 or 20, from my earlier relationship with a girlfriend was also traveling with us. We had drugs to see us up and back.

We got a hotel in Mississauga and decided to go to Niagara Falls. That night Karen wasn't feeling well and laid on the bed. After we watched the news, I felt the bed shaking and Karen was going in and out of consciousness. She had bad pain in her head like it was being split open with an axe. Panic set in and I didn't know what to do. I went into the washroom and got a wet facecloth with cold water. I put it on her head. She was crying and freaking out and walking up and down the hallway. I knew something was drastically wrong and I knew if she passed out she would die. All I could think of doing was keeping her moving. My son phoned security. They came up and didn't know what to do either so they phoned an ambulance and they took her to the Mississauga Hospital.

They kept her for a couple of days. My son and I were free floating and went to see The Rolling Stones that night. We came back to the hospital the next day and they said they were going to let her out. They'd found out she was a druggie and it seemed they didn't have the same interest in her as they did the day before. She lied to get out of hospital and told them she was better. She wasn't better. She was just scared and didn't want to be in the hospital in Mississauga when her home was a thousand miles away.

It took us two days traveling to get home. She was sick all the way. She didn't get much sleep. She tried smoking marijuana to make her feel better but it didn't help. I took her in the hospital about 10 o'clock that night. The next morning she went into labour and had our daughter, Lacie Jade, who we found out later was born a cocaine addict.

A few days later, Karen had a stroke and soon after that she had another. After the second stroke, I asked the nurse who the woman was in my wife's bed. I was sure she wasn't my wife. I told the nurse there was something drastically wrong with her. They moved her down to the psychiatric ward of the hospital. Friday was business as usual for me. I thought Karen would be better and I would take her home. I later found out that they had been calling the house, trying to get hold of me all day because she'd had another stroke.

I got there and her parents were there as well as John and Shirley, a Christian couple that had really been a witness for us, in looking after Jennifer while we were in jail. Karen was laying in bed and looked fine but she wasn't. She had gone into a vegetable state. They had a psychiatrist and a psychologist examine her and they didn't know what to think. I was crushed. I lay on the bed with her and cried my heart out. It was such a hopeless, helpless situation. I didn't know what would become of my wife. They were going to send her to St. John Hospital because there was nothing more they could do for her.

At that point I realized that I wanted to contact a friend of mine from my past, Rusty Sullivan. He had come back to the Lord and I felt he was like my hotline to God. It's interesting how we think of God when times are really rough. When things are good He's not really on our mind. I called Rusty and he could tell something was wrong. I told him about Karen. He came immediately and said, "I don't want them to ship her to St. John before I pray". He went into the room and prayed over her. We left as they prepared to take her to the ambulance.

I walked around outside the hospital, rolled a joint and got stoned, because that's how I dealt with life. Rusty told me he had never felt the presence of God like he had when he was in the room with Karen. He said he didn't really know what happened, but he knew God had met him during that prayer. They loaded Karen into the ambulance and Rusty said he'd take me to St. John. We had to go and pick up his wife Mary, and then we headed out. Karen was in Intensive Care and I ended up talking to a specialist, Peter Bailey. He didn't know the whole situation and assured me that she was not going to die. She would probably live through the night.

Rusty and Mary took me home to Tracy. On the way a lot of things were going through my mind. Mary shared the Lord with me. Now I knew the Lord before, but she told me that I was at a crossroads in life and the decision that I made would determine my future. Looking back now, she was right. My life was definitely at a crossroads.

I believe God lets circumstances happen to us to bring us to a place where we have to make a choice. He won't make it for us. During the trip my whole life flashed before my eyes. Thoughts ran through my mind; like my wife being in a mental institution for the rest of her life; me taking the kids there on the weekend to visit her, and them growing up without a mother. How would I explain our selfishness, our drive to party and look out for number one with no value or concern for them. I realized how devastating and unfair that would be on my children. It's ironic that one has to come to a place of crashing and burning out to realize that there's more to life than meets the eye.

My baby was just born and still in the hospital. Jennifer, Meaghan and Samantha were with Karen's parents. My kids had toy boxes full of toys, name brand clothes, and good food. I thought I was doing great to give my kids a life without poverty. I hadn't given them any life at all. What I began to discover was that, all my children really wanted was a Dad. They didn't want to live in the crazy household I created. I got home about 2 a.m. and was all alone. I recall standing in the driveway and looking up at the sky and talking to the Lord and saying, "Jesus if you are real and if you'll heal my wife and send her home to raise my children, I'll serve you".

Then I went in the house and went to bed. The next day I hooked up with my friend Bert and went to visit my wife. I had an opportunity to talk with Dr. Peter Bailey again. He took me to the Quiet Room. That is where they lay the heavy on you, tell you the deal. They told me my wife had the mind of a primitive child. She had no control of her bowels or kidneys. They had her in a diaper. She had no motor skills. Her hands were bound up like boxing gloves in gauze and tied to the side of the bed because anything she picked up she put in her mouth. So that's where the three strokes from the cocaine abuse had left her. We still had a baby in the Fredericton Hospital.

The next day Bert and I met up with a guy named Dan Sheridan at the shopping mall. Bert had previously met Dan and Bert told me he could heal my wife. I explained the situation to Dan and he said, "Do you want to go outside and pray?" I said we could just pray where we were.

At that same time there was a prayer meeting going on at a house in Tracy, at Mike and Anne MacLean's. They knew who I was, a drug dealer, and had heard that the drug dealer's wife had had a couple of strokes and was in the St. John Hospital. They were praying that God would somehow intercede, heal my wife and win us to Jesus. Here's Dan who prays for my wife and after that heads to that very same prayer group. When he got there late he apologized and told them that he was praying with me. Everyone began to laugh and told him that they also had been praying that we would allow God to intervene in our lives, even though we were drug dealers. Only God could put that together.

For the next 14 days I went to the hospital and had neighbours looking after my children. The baby, Lacie Jade had come home from the hospital and a family was looking after her. My in-laws helped look after the children as well, to give me the freedom to visit my wife. I spent eight to twelve hours a day by her bedside and for the most part there was no conversation. She didn't even know where she was. The only communication we had was this little chin wave. I would put my hand under my chin and wave and she would wave back. That was the only language we had!

One day they decided to put her on a treadmill. I came in to visit with my son. She got off the bed and walked to the bathroom. I was amazed. I asked her how she was able to walk. She told me about going to the treadmill in a wheelchair and fifteen minutes later, they said, "Lady there's nothing wrong with you", and sent her back upstairs. While she was telling me this, I was mindful of the prayer we'd prayed with Dan and the prayer I'd prayed the night before. I knew in my heart that the Lord had healed her.

Four or five days later, we walked out of the hospital, arm in arm and came home. I told her that I believed God had healed her. That Sunday we went to church and sat in the back. I don't know what the service was about, but I was touched by the Holy Spirit. I just sat and cried through the whole service. Here's the big, tough drug dealer from down the road, the plague of their community, just crying. I knew when I got out of my seat at the end of the service and shook the Pastor's hand, I felt like a ton of weight had been lifted off my shoulders. I could have just floated out the door.

In the process of all that was happening, I had assumed that Karen had felt the same thing. I began to find out a few days later that it wasn't true. She had been to church. She had been healed, but she hadn't really dedicated her life. The following Thursday I went to a dealer's house because the guy owed me some money. I went to pick it up. I still had debts to be paid even though I was a Christian. For the first four to six weeks I was saved I dealt drugs because I didn't know what else to do to make a living, but the Lord convicted me. I quit dealing and began depending on Him. When you come out of the drug world and the hierarchy I was in, you don't have any alternative but to take the stuff, sell it and pay them off. I knew that I had to do that. I believe the Lord gave me the grace and protection to do it. I don't believe it is what He wanted me to do but I was released to do it.

I came back that night and Kathy, an old girlfriend of mine, was home with Karen helping out with the new baby. Karen was very moody when I got home and later that evening she told me she wished I had brought home some cocaine. Here I was tying up the loose ends. I couldn't believe my ears.

Later that evening, I took Karen for a drive to talk about what she had said. I asked her, "What about me and the children?" She said she didn't care about me or the children. She just knew that if she had done cocaine and died, she would be out of here. She wouldn't have to worry about anything else. Life would be over. I told her life wouldn't be over, it would be just starting. I told her life begins at death and told her about eternal life. I began to share scriptures with her that the Lord had given me, and through that process of talking and sharing, I led my wife to the Lord. She rededicated her life to Jesus Christ in the front seat of my car, in a gravel pit in Beaver Dam. So you can see God can meet you anywhere. I believe Satan was speaking through my wife that night trying to convince her to kill herself. That was the about-turn in Karen's life.

A week or two later, we went to a Baptist Bible study. Then I heard Monty Lewis was speaking at the Smythe Street Cathedral. We went and when Monty was finished preaching my wife and I and Bert and Susan went up to the altar and recommitted our lives to Jesus Christ. We went back that night because we were looking for a place to go to Church. I'd realized that I was tired of running my life my way and telling my wife what to do. We wanted God to tell us where to go and had asked Him for a sign. That night, Lorna Hashey, a Pastor's wife came up to me after the service. She wanted to know if my wife would be embarrassed if she gave her a bag or two of clothes. I told her I didn't think so. They were beautiful clothes and Karen took them home. They fit her to a tee. We believe that this was God's way of showing us that He wanted us to go to Smythe Street Cathedral.

A new journey begins. We are into our thirteenth year in that church. We were baptized in water. Our children were saved and baptized. I was now 43 years old. I had spent 32 years living on the street using drugs and alcohol and I was a career criminal, a violent aggressor, thief, and shoplifter. I never spent a lot of time in prison but a lot of time on the streets. I accumulated a lot of pain, hurt, shame, guilt, unworthiness and low self esteem. I don't share that stuff pridefully. I am actually ashamed of the person I'd become and the things that I did. I share them to give a witness for Jesus Christ, of just how powerful He is to change my life. Jesus can turn anyone's life around. Just give Him a chance.

For 25 years, I was deceived by the devil. I believed a lie, that Jesus died a horrible death on the cross only for good people to go to heaven. I have since found out that Jesus died for everybody. Scriptures like Romans 3:23 "All have sinned and fallen short of the glory of God", showed me that I am part of the "all". I found out the criteria for going to heaven is simply that I have to be a sinner because Jesus died for sinners. I found out the first person into heaven was a thief on the cross. I found out that it is not keeping the law but the cross that gets us into heaven. The Bible says, "By grace you are saved, through faith" (Ephesians 2:8). I found out that salvation is a gift and I'm thankful for it. God is willing to give this gift to anyone.

He healed our baby Lacie Jade who was born with a cocaine addiction. We were treating her for colic when we found out about birth mothers who had used cocaine. So I did what the Bible in the book of James told us to do and that was call the elders of the church and pray for healing. The elders gathered and laid hands on her and she was totally healed. She is twelve years old today and smart as a whip. There were no repercussions and she does well in school. God is good!

In the early months of my newfound faith in Jesus Christ. I was looking for a new direction in life and was trying to figure out how to raise my four girls. My wife had been healed. I had been delivered. We started going to church and building relationships with Monty and Lynda Lewis from the "Cons for Christ" Prison Ministry. Monty's an ex-offender himself. We started going to a mid-week Bible Study at Mike and Ann McLean's house, with Bert and Susan, Jim and Joanne who were all new Christians. Mike taught on how to be a Christian without being religious. This was the place I first learned to pray out loud.

I knew I couldn't go back to the street, I'd done that before and fell back. I was able to hang out with those working at "Cons for Christ" and helped stamp books. They distribute books to over 69 different prisons across Canada. I knew that these people were making it and if I hung out there, I'd make it too. Positive fellowship is important.

I never fellowshipped with people in the church when I made my first commitment to Christ, so I went back to fellowshipping with the world. I didn't want to make that mistake again. I believe fellowship is a key. There are actually three keys, one is the Word, one is prayer and the other is fellowship with other believers. I started hanging out at Smythe Street Cathedral doing the books and working with guys like Monty Lewis and Gene Ross. I just wanted to stay clean. I just wanted to make it. I'd attempted this before and never made it. It was a whole new thing.

I had a Harley Davidson at the time and I got interested in bike ministry ICBA (International Christian Bikers Association). They had done a movie called "God Rides A Harley". I had seen this movie during a drug deal years ago and had the thought then, that I could do that and wear Christian colours. I never thought about wearing outlaw colours but Christian colours were a different story. Gene and I began talking about starting a bike chapter. He came up with the name Kingdom Riders. We started the chapter and at one time we had about 20 riders. Our jackets had a white cross on the back and "born again" and John 3:3. We got involved in prison ministry with Monty and did some bike ministry. It lasted about two years and we had to set it aside due to conflicts of interest.

As a result I looked up some material from the Christian Motorcycle Association and decided I would join them as an independent person. Karen and I began to ride with them and have been with them since 1991. We started a chapter here and I was the president for several years. Then I became the chaplain for the chapter. I worked to help start another CMA chapter in Moncton, N.B.. Now we're working to get one started in Miramachi, St. John and Grand Falls area. God is faithful. If you'll do the possible, God will do the impossible. We believe we need Christian bikers across the Provinces, in every city to bring glory to God and a witness to the biker gangs.

We were living on welfare but we were keeping up. It wasn't like having the money we were used to, but we got by. For the first twelve to fourteen months of my new life, I was involved every day and every night with something. We had a Bible study for new Christians where we studied the book "How To Be A Christian Without Being Religious" by Fritz Reiner. Every noonhour I would go in and hang out with the Community Chaplain and others downtown. Andrew Hachey was Chaplain at that time. On Friday nights, there was a group called "New Wine", a twelve-step group based on the Bible, using illustrations from Oswald Chambers book, "My Utmost For His Highest". On Saturday nights, there was the Tracy Fellowship which was a non-denominational fellowship. On Sunday morning and evening, there was church service at the Smythe Street church which became our home church.

When I wasn't out at all these functions, I would be in the basement where I would study the Bible. For many months, I spent eight to twelve hours a day with the Word. The reason for all that was a fear that I would fall away. After all I had done that before and the price we paid was way too high. I didn't want to end up there again.

A couple of years later, I was clean and saved and doing all the things I talked about, but I wanted to do something more with my life. One night Karen met with a woman to look into going to St. Thomas University, so I went with her. I sat in her living room as they discussed the University. I listened and thought that's what I'd like to do. The next day my wife and I were on the grounds of St. Thomas University in Fredericton, NB. I was a Grade eight dropout, although I did get my GED in prison. We didn't know what we wanted to be, we just decided to go. We were accepted on a probationary process for six months. We took three courses the first year. We didn't take a full course load the first year because we didn't think we could handle it, and because we were so involved in other areas.

This was a whole new reality. We were meeting new friends and we were 'heavy' then and now with Christian T-shirts and sharing the Gospel and Jesus. We shared our story with both professors and students. In my third year my marks were really high and I decided I wanted to take Sociology. I knew that if I wanted to be a Sociologist, the next two years would be tough. I would have to really zero in. My wife decided to take Sociology as well. It was the longest goal I had ever made. I started by setting small goals, like reaching mid-term. Well, I got to mid term and got good marks. Then I worked towards Christmas. I'd made it half way. The end of the first year I had passed and I was excited. Karen and I had both made it, quite a feat when you haven't amounted to anything your whole life.

God pulled us through that first year and helped us to see the reality that we could do anything. God has given me two specific scriptures regarding this: Philippians 4:13 "I can do all things through Christ who strengthens me". I just stand on that verse. I believe it. I utilize it and I share it with others. The other verse is Philippians 1:6 "He who began a good work in you will bring it to completion". I knew God had started something and He was seeing it through.

We graduated. I have to thank God for the staying power of Jesus Christ through His Holy Spirit. He influenced me, strengthened me and guided me in this and all the other volunteer things I was involved in through those years. We both graduated with Honors Degrees hoping that someday we can go on to a Master's level.

In the fourth year of University, there was opportunity to do a resume for chaplaincy job in St. John, N.B. I never really anticipated getting the job. I'd never done a resume before and I was in my last year of University. I'd never had a real, legal job. They chose another person for the job. Then they called me back and and said there was some conflict with the other person and as a result, I got the job. I believe God sent me. I had never intended to go there. I never liked St. John as it was a big and dirty city. I got my first paid position as the Saint John Community Chaplain. I have now been there seven years.

I remember my first day on the job. This guy came in and he was really drunk. He was cursing and swearing and tearing me down. Well, the flesh rose up in me being an old street fighter. But another thought came to me which I know was the Lord speaking to me and very quietly said, "why did he come?" I began pondering that thought and wondered why did he come. We didn't have drugs or alcohol here. As a result I listened to the Lord and that was the beginning of my working with this guy. He was three years getting sober. I spent a lot of time with him and there was a lot of frustration. I thank the Lord now as Bob has graduated with a criminology degree with a B+ average. He has already been accepted into St. Mary's University to do his Masters Degree. An alcoholic and ex-offender like myself, but God in His mercy and grace showed me something in this guy, even at the very beginning.

I thank God today that I listened to the Holy Spirit and not to my own flesh. That was one of the many challenges at the St. John Chaplaincy. It has not been without stress and frustration, but it is still a blessing. I try to build relationships with people to help them. I believe Jesus built relationships and I believe that is what Jesus is all about. He did build a wonderful relationship with me and my family, and as a result, we are all serving him today. That's my desire, to build a relationship with each and every person I meet. The people that I work with have broken dreams, broken realities, broken lives and broken homes. They have experienced drugs, alcohol, sexual, verbal and physical abuse and many other things. The only way that they know how to deal with them is through band-aid solutions. Satan gives band-aid solutions. It is only God that can heal and restore the little boy and the little girl that has been wounded. Once God has healed our inner child, He can use us to help others in the same way.

I guess that is what I'm all about, allowing God to use me. He is continually restoring me and healing me and working on the child within. From years of living on the street, drugs and alcohol, and all that crazy lifestyle, you don't come out of that on your own. We confess our faith to Jesus Christ and accept Him into our heart. We have salvation and our eternity is intact. Yet we still need the healing within from our past and only Jesus can do that.

I have had the opportunity to appear on the 100 Huntley Street T.V. program a number of times, once with my wife. We have done several videos locally. In 1999 we had a video done with Pat Robertson and the 700 Club, "Operation Blessing". Now we are telling our story through this book. We are excited about the opportunities God has given us to speak in churches and schools, and wherever God allows us entry. About five years ago, I was ordained through the Apostolic Church of Pentecost. Who would have believed that a drug-dealing tough guy could become a Minister of the Gospel! With God, all things are possible. (Matt. 19:26).

The Saint John Community Chaplaincy ministry has grown tremendously over the years. Our greatest need is for workers. I'm convinced God's not done with me yet, I believe He's only just started. I believe there is a lot of work to do. I have a desire to go back to school and do some writing down the road. My desire is to write a book someday. I believe in the Biblical model of restorative justice. The Provincial and Federal Governments are moving towards community corrections and realizing that there are other options rather than incarceration. I'm an advocate of that. I want to utilize the principles of the Bible. I want to help people to see that the problems of drugs and alcohol are merely symptoms. Jesus wants to look at the heart and I want to help secular organizations to look at the heart too.

There's much more to be done. There's a lot of new people to meet, a lot of hurting people, and people still in prison. I thank God that I have an opportunity to go to the institutions that house these people, work with them and help make a difference in people's lives. (Matthew 18: 18-20).

Perhaps you have been reading my story and don't believe that God loves you and Jesus died for you. I believed that lie of the devil for over 25 years. I believed in God and that Jesus died for good people and I wasn't a good person. I never questioned the reality of God, I just believed I wasn't good enough. I didn't understand mercy and grace. I thought I had to earn my way to heaven. I'm glad that Jesus revealed the truth to me about that lie. He paid the price and all I had to do was accept, in faith, what had already been done for me by Christ. It's free for us but it cost Jesus His life. (John 17:4)

Dave can be contacted at:

The Saint John Community Chaplaincy
36 Sewell Street,
Saint John, New Brunswick E2L 3A2

Dave Hardy

'Our first summer' Millbrook 1980 Dave and Karen

Dave Hardy – 1982
Recovering from bike accident

Dave in Spring Hill Institution - 1983

Bride – Karen Hardy Sept. 28, 1985

*Dave and Karen Hardy, Jennifer, Meaghan,
Lacie, and Samantha*

Coke Kills!

The Life
of
KAREN HARDY

Ben and I went over the border to the U.S. We looked like a couple. We went to the dealer's house, picked up the drugs and drove back to Calais. The plan was all worked out with Dave. I was to drop Ben off and he was to walk back across the train bridge and I'd pick him up on the other side. He was in a hurry and asked me to put the drugs in the back of my jeans and drive across the border. I said if anything happens to me, you'll hear it from Dave. Ben said he would take full responsibility. We got to the Milltown border and the police came from everywhere. They told us we were under arrest and they took us to the St. Stephen's border. Ben was taken to a cell, while I was put in a room to be strip searched by two female officers.

It appeared that I had everything going for me. I was adopted as a baby by good parents who really loved me. I had a brother, eight years older than me and a sister four years older than me. They were also adopted . We were three kids from three different cities. One was from Fredericton, one was from Saint John and one was from Woodstock, New Brunswick, a province in Eastern Canada.

We lived in a nice four bedroom home on Princess Court in Marysville. As a child, I was a tomboy. We had a fence around the front yard with an arbour over it. My parents told me, that one day, they came out, looked and couldn't see me and there I was on top of the arbour. They told me I dug a hole under the fence and ran across the road behind my best friend's house up over the hill. My parents did their best with all three of us. We never lacked for anything. We went to Florida every year. We had snowmobiles. I had a dirt bike. I wore the very best clothes. I was the baby so I got pretty much what I wanted.

I began figure skating quite young and really loved it. My parents went above and beyond the call of duty to help me succeed in life. I took lessons for seven to eight years and really excelled in it and enjoyed it. I was in special events - Christmas and holiday presentations. In one I was a tree, in another I was a court jester. We were all in costumes. We had so much fun and freedom. Our religious denomination did not allow us to dance. I had always wanted to dance and figure skate. It was an outlet for me. Although I was not allowed to go to dances, I was free to dance on skates.

One thing I never really liked was the competitions. After I'd been in skating for a few years I earned several badges and trophies. The competitions that they wanted me involved in, I shied away from. I've never been one to compete against another, probably because I never felt like I was as good as others. Things that happened really put a lot of garbage in my mind that I couldn't process mentally or emotionally at the time. I never understood why I felt the way I did about things.

My parents got me SK figure skates and I still have them to this day. I remember back then that the boots had to be ordered separately from the blade and they were well over $200, even then. They were professional and had the steel shanks and straps in the sides for ankle support. I never wore them long enough to break them in. I was like that with a lot of things. Every time the novelty of something wore off I didn't want to do it anymore. It had to be new and exciting (whether sports, a toy, clothes, a snowmobile, or a motorbike).

We used to go to Prince Edward Island, an island off the coast of New Brunswick, every summer. I remember going to see the Anne of Green Gables play and her house. My parents would rent a cottage and we would go to Cavendish Beach. They took me to the capital of PEI - Charlottetown. At our cottage in the summer, my mom would read me Anne of Green Gables late at night. I would climb into bed with her and she would read me a chapter or two of the book. Those were such special times.

When I went to Kindergarten, I remember how I got there. I took a city transit bus at the end of Canada Street in the morning, about half a mile from our home in Marysville. Mom would walk me to the stop and would wait until the bus picked me up. I really enjoyed it. I felt like a big girl going on a bus to kindergarten.

The following year I went to Marysville School for Grade One. My teacher was Mrs. King. I really looked up to her. She represented a female authority figure and a responsible person in my life and I really loved her. I remember near the end of Grade One she got popsicles for everyone and was asking what color everyone wanted. It ended up that I didn't want orange and that was all that was left. She called me a spoiled brat and I remember the rejection I felt, because I looked up to her so much. Maybe I had been given all I wanted at home and she might have had a reason to think that way, but it broke my heart. We grow up saying things like "sticks and stones will break my bones but names will never hurt me", but that's not true. Being called a spoiled brat really hurt me.

In elementary school I was always for the underdog. There was a guy in our school who had to wear a helmet on the playground, George Clark. I heard he had been struck by a car so he had to wear the helmet. He definitely had mental deficiencies, but I felt bad for him because the kids made fun of him and called him names. I tried to be nice and that got me into a situation where George started following me around because I gave him attention. He thought I cared about him in a deeper way than I did. It was difficult because him following me caused the children to tease me as well.

The sexual abuse started so young, I think I was approximately three or four years old. I approached my sister to talk about the abuse about five years ago as I was really in torment. It did things to me that I didn't know how to deal with. Looking back, I guess it's easier to understand why I made

84

some of the decisions and choices I did. They were an attempt to medicate the emotional pain I was experiencing.

It all started when my parents left me with the babysitter. He would take me down to a room in the basement. I wonder to this day what he told me that made me so scared that I never told. I knew it was wrong. I believe that's an inherent thing God puts in each one of us, but I never said a word.

When he touched me in certain ways my body would respond. I believe that's how God created our bodies for sexual pleasure and that it is natural to respond. Yet in the very act, I knew in my mind, even as small child, that what was being done was wrong. I couldn't understand why some of the touches felt good. I took on a lot of guilt and shame over experiencing a pleasurable sensation when I knew it was wrong. This continued from three to eight years of age. When I was young, after the abuse had begun, I'd lay in bed screaming. I thought there were entities in my room.

I wonder about my grandma who had an apartment downstairs in our house. She loved me and was very protective of us. She was from England and was very old school. I loved her. She taught me how to knit. She'd make me boiled eggs in neat little egg cups. I spent lots of time there. Looking back now, I remember that she never got along with my babysitter. I wonder if she knew what happened when my parents left me with him because we had to go downstairs and past her apartment to get to the room in the basement.

Sexual abuse was hush hush in the late 60's and early 70's. Maybe I'm off the wall but I wonder if that's why they didn't get along. I'll never know because she passed away a while ago. But I know in everything that happened, God can use it for His glory. I hope, pray, and trust in God that He will use my story to help set other women free from the bondage of sin that the enemy gets us in.

Looking back at my own behaviour and how I acted out sexually, it's easy to see the signs now. I know there was a problem with abuse but back then it wasn't talked about. I know if my children exhibited the same behaviour, I would automatically think there was abuse going on.

I remember once I got very angry. I flew into rages as a young child. I kicked a hole in the hallway wall. I wondered why I never told Mom and Dad what was going on. When I took it to my sister five or six years ago, she came with me to see my parents. I wanted them to see that it wasn't their fault that I made some of the decisions I had. I chose rebellion and I wanted them to see they had done the best they could. I was hoping it would help them understand my choices. It wasn't because they were bad parents or didn't go the extra mile. I still wonder if they understood what I was trying to say.

Even with my abuser, God is taking me through different levels. I remember the many emotional states I have gone through and the different healing work God has done in me. I have gone from being totally irate and hating him, to feeling compassion and sadness in my heart. God has allowed me to see that something drastic and devastating must have happened to him because what he did to me was not normal behaviour. I haven't had the courage to confront him yet. All in God's time. He will give me the necessary strength.

As I was growing up in Marysville, I was always at the swimming pool in the summer months. I was a member of the diving club and I took diving and swimming lessons. I swam every day. If the pool was open, I'd be there. I think back to different things that happened there, and much of it was inappropriate behaviour. I would not call it inappropriate sexual behaviour, because as a child, any sexual behaviour is inappropriate. I remember playing doctor at the pool with a boy and letting him touch my private parts because I wanted him to like me which seemed to work for a while. I felt very dirty when confronted. I don't remember what was said but it felt like another nail of rejection.

We used to go to Grand Mannan quite a bit. My parents knew lots of people. My biggest problem was that I didn't feel like I fit in anywhere, until I started hanging around older kids. It probably had something to do with the fact that my innocence had been stolen at such a young age.

My parents were very heavily involved in the church and were going to prayer group. There was a group of girls in my church that I could have played with but I preferred the older kids. We used to sing special numbers in church every two or three months. There was four of us - Marilyn, Robyn, Gail and me. I was in the children's choir group. I also went to youth group and church twice on Sundays.

We used to spend lots of time at the cottage at the church

campgrounds in the summer, until my teen years. I went to kid's camp, youth camp and every year I would have an experience with the Lord, but I couldn't seem to follow through. This dark secret kept gnawing away at me. I felt dirty and believed Jesus couldn't forgive me.

I remember being at the cottage in grade 7 or 8 and I got my first LSD (acid). I got it from a PK (Preacher's Kid). I was acting tough and said, "I do that all the time". An hour or so later when I began to hallucinate, I was terrified. I ran down to the front of the campground next to the water thinking the waves were chasing me. I remember going back to the cottage and I wanted a drink. I set the cup on the cupboard and poured the milk. I missed the cup and poured the entire quart on the cupboard. I guess you learn to fake it and lie and cover up for all your insecurities. I continued to do that and became a person I didn't even know. The problem was I didn't really have an identity, it had been stolen.

Around the same time, my Mom and Dad were involved in Amway. They used to have lots of meetings at the house. Dad had a stock room downstairs. I used to help him sort and stock shelves and keep records. I met lots of people. A couple from McAdam had two daughters. The oldest, Meaghan, was the same age as me and we became friends. All the time I carried the secret of my abuse. I never felt that I fit in with them.

My father owned a laundromat and I worked there for a while on Fridays. My Uncle had a storage warehouse that was beside the laundromat. My cousin Andrew worked there. One day I was supposed to be at the laundromat working, but I was at the warehouse with my cousin Andrew. His father had these golf carts he used in the warehouse and we rode these carts. We got caught by our fathers.

When I was younger, my sister and I did lots of housework, but I preferred to help my Dad in the yard, piling wood. My father was an avid gardener. He had the most beautiful garden. I liked being outside because inside I felt closed in with all that was going on in my subconscious.

I played little league for at least two years. Jennifer and I were the only two girls in the whole league. We were on two different teams. I was on the Legionnaires team. I loved sports especially baseball. I didn't want any dresses or Barbies.

Most years we would go to Florida as a family. One year we took a trip to Boston. I loved baseball live or on T.V. Dad bought tickets, as a surprise, for the playoff game, Boston Red Sox against the Cincinnati Reds. I still have the cap from that game. My uncle and cousin came too. It was a really big deal. I lived a privileged childhood in an above-average income family. My parents didn't know how the years of sexual abuse would affect all areas of my life.

The first boy I dated was Kevin Brown. He was my first true love. He was so kind, not pushy or demanding. I was 12 or 13. He never pressured me or used me. I heard ten years later that he died in a plane crash. Grandma McMillan who lived downstairs at our home died too. The finality of death struck me. I had just rededicated my life to the Lord.

In junior high I had a teacher who lived close to our home. He was married with one son. His wife asked me to babysit and I felt special. They came home late and suggested I stay over in the spare room. Some time in the night I woke up and heard a noise. My teacher was in the room. The next thing I knew the door flew open and his wife came in and caught him in the room with me. I'm not 100% sure what would have happened or why he was there but I have a good idea. They had a big fight about how could she trust him. I never babysat for them again.

My gym teacher, in Grade Seven was so handsome and I had crush on him. I was totally crushed when I found out he was dating the math teacher. One day in gym class another girl and I were getting balls in the equipment room. The gym teacher and another teacher were also in there. Suddenly the lights went out. The room went black and I felt hands all over me. I screamed and so did the other girl. Another molestation. Now I thought my gym teacher was garbage. It started to strengthen my negative beliefs of men.

I got angry at my father very often. I don't know why. I told him when I grew up I was going to marry a man who would be home in the evenings. Dad was a great provider, but he was gone a lot. As a result of my experiences with male figures, I began to form ideals of men.

The teacher in the equipment room was the Head of the Department and a member of a group going on a train trip to Moncton. It was my first time on a train and I felt very independent. We stayed in a hotel. The teacher made moves on me during the trip. Situations like that made me feel like a sex object - to be used for gratification. It was part of the reinforcement that I was to be used. I took on a different mind set. Looking back I can't say when I crossed the threshold but all these little things that happened started to build up. I was filled with negative feelings and I hated myself. I don't know exactly when it started, but I thought I was garbage. I started spiraling out of control.

When I was 14 I had a boyfriend named Trevor. I desperately wanted people to like me. Satan doesn't care how long it takes to destroy life, he just wants to do it. He's so sneaky and sly that you are totally unaware. He had me doomed for failure from the time I was three years old. I was promiscuous from thirteen. I just assumed you were sexual by then. I was at Trevor's one day and his Dad came to visit and caught us in bed, not having sex but similar behaviours. I thought I was just being a good girlfriend.

Marysville was a small community and there was not much to do. In Grade five and six , I went to the YMCA for swimming, doing gym and playing ball. This was an attempt to keep me occupied so I wouldn't get into trouble. We went to my friend's house because her Mom smoked. Now I was smoking marijuana on a regular basis and using alcohol. When there was a dry spell, we sniffed "Pam" spray in a plastic bag. We did magic mushrooms. We would try anything. We experienced some bad hallucinations.

One of my friends had a brother who I had crush on. He forced me to have sex with him in their basement. I never thought of it as rape then. Then her grandfather, got into bed with me when I stayed over, and started feeling me. I thought "you dirty old man". I wanted to wash it all off. I felt so dirty. Only Jesus can wash us clean. Sexual abuse became a lifestyle.

I had a false sense of security which helped reinforce where I was headed in the next 12 years. I was on a slippery slope. I was playing in Satan's domain. He isn't up front, he's sneaky. He provides quick cures and immediate gratification through behaviors, attitudes, drugs and alcohol. I never imagined one joint would lead me to the point of near death in September of 1989. I began smoking marijuana at the graveyard beside the school. The first time, I smoked, at thirteen was with four friends, Susan, Sherry, Nicole and Heidi. I felt acceptance and belonging with these older girls. Once, there was a traveling zoo in town with animals in Kings Place. I went through the mall being silly, talking about how the lion ate our friend.

I did well in school until then. In Grade 7, I got 100% on a French exam. I was so proud. The same year my grades slipped and I stopped caring. Marijuana takes your drive and initiative away. I was a cheerleader and in Junior varsity volleyball. By Grade 8 it all stopped. For Junior High I had to take a school bus to the city to George Street High. My lunch money was spent on dope before school. During breaks, lunch and after school, I smoked. In High School some of the teachers attempted to straighten me out.

My friends and I went to Millbrook to party. One of the girls made out with a married guy and his wife caught them. He had attempted to rape her. Many bad things happened there. Coming home one night, the same guy grabbed me and raped me. I went home feeling dirty and tried to wash. I cried and thought "God why me?". I never got an answer!

Shortly after, I met Dave Hardy. I told him I would never go out with him. He was the most arrogant, male chauvinist I had ever met, but he was a big man in the drug scene. Wherever he went, he was smoking, rolling, selling. Something about him was enticing. I found myself in places where he was. One day we were in the park and he was rolling joints and passing them around. He asked if I wanted a ride home. I got in his truck and he made a pass at me. We got to my brother's place. My parents were away in Florida. I had a small black and white T.V. that I decided I wanted to take home, so I asked if he'd drive me home with it. It was 2:30 a.m. I had learned a lot about control and manipulation and that was my way of getting what I wanted. He said "Okay". I invited him in and we sat on the couch on opposite ends. He said "Are you going to sit there all night?" He spent the night. That was the beginning of my chasing after him for a long time.

I was aware he had two other girlfriends but hanging with him was a free stone. He had lots of money and I thought he was cool. We spent most of our time getting high and having sex. Within a year of my first spending the night with him, I had my first child, Jennifer born January 22, 1982. At that point Dave was around, but he was living the way he wanted to live. He made no commitment to me but I wanted to win his favor.

We continued to date but it was a crazy lifestyle. He became abusive. In 1982 he was in a motorcycle accident and was in the hospital. He got two pins in his knee and a cast on his leg. He got mad at the doctor in the hospital and signed himself out. While he was laid up, he had a partner in the drug scene. Arrangements had been for me to drive his partner over the border, on this specific night, and make a pick-up from a U.S. dealer. Then I was to drop him off. I was not to be involved in any moving of drugs at any time. Things didn't turn out the way we planned. Apparently, the house had been bugged by the police and they had recorded us inside the house and on the phone. They planted the bugs on the day Dave was in the accident. They knew a deal was going down and they followed us over the border. We went to a drive-through bank in Calais, Maine changing our money into American. I was to go with Dave's partner and just drop him off. It was only back on the Canadian side that I would see him again. Ben changed the plans. When we arrived at the border, the police were everywhere.

During the drive from the Milltown border to St. Stephen, the police made me put my hands on the back of the front seat so I couldn't remove any coke or hash from my back pocket. When I got into the room for the search, they asked me if I had anything I wanted to give them. I said "Yes, I have an ounce of hash and weed". The ounce of cocaine had been wrapped in masking tape so you couldn't see inside. They put me in a room with five cops and told me I would lose my child and spend seven years in jail for importing drugs. The police told me that Ben was in a cell laughing because he knew I would take the rap for everything. Dave had told me, "If anything ever goes wrong don't say anything". I told them I wanted to see a lawyer. The officer in charge, the head of narcotics, took my purse. I still have it today. She threw it at me, telling me I would get seven years in prison.

I was terrified. They took Ben and I in a police car to

Fredericton after the interrogations. I was locked in a cold cell. I had been living on the wrong side of the law by having Dave as a boyfriend. I had put myself in many precarious situations, but this was the first time I was really alone. They gave me my winter coat to use as a pillow. I didn't sleep much that night. They took us into court the next morning and we were released on a written undertaking. The journey began of finding a lawyer to represent me. I went through five different lawyers. The police had bugged the house and had the tapes. Each lawyer wanted me to identify the voices on them but I refused.

Finally I went to court and the judge told me if I didn't have a lawyer by my next appearance, he would appoint one for me. I was going to get a new lawyer the night before court. It was my last chance. I walked into the lawyer's office and there were two RCMP officers there. He told them he wouldn't represent me unless I identified the voices on the tape. I ran out of there crying. I was at a loss and didn't know what to do. I got a lawyer who didn't deal with criminal cases, just property. The first day of my trial I had my mom's car. By this time Dave had moved from Harvey to Tracy and was living with Kathy. I was going to pick them up and was nervous since I had no previous encounters with courts or anything of that nature.

I had been scared to go home when we had been busted, because my parents would be devastated. I finally went home and we decided to try to make it through the best we could. Mom and Dad couldn't come to court because they were too upset. There was a couple, John and Shirley Schriver, who had been youth leaders at Church. They had always been there and had never given up on me. They were the two people who would show me unconditional love. I would call them at 3 or 4 a.m. wasted and John would leave his home and come all the way to Marysville to pick me up. It was a 15 to 20 minute drive. He would take me back to their house and Shirley would have coffee waiting and they would listen. They were the ones, that when the judge sentenced me to jail, were there to look after my daughter Jennifer, who was one year old. They brought her to visit me. My parents came to visit me as well.

I had migraines from stress for the first two weeks and I

was sick and vomiting. I went to the doctor in jail, which was the same doctor I knew from on the street. After the drug bust, my name was in the paper. I went to this doctor because I couldn't sleep. He gave me a lecture and told me I shouldn't have been in that situation. What was I doing with a man so much older and devastating my parents. He told me I was a drug addict and had to start dealing with some of my issues. I rebelled against that and wanted nothing to do with him. Here he was the prison doctor. I didn't want to hear what he told me.

One day while I was in jail, they took us to Gagetown military base on an outing. I didn't care where I was, I was so thankful to get out of prison for the day. Some young girls I did time with cursed and complained the whole time. They planned on getting out and getting pregnant so they could get full welfare. I felt so angry at them. I had a child that I was separated from, and they had no idea what it was like. While pregnant, I thought I would have this cute baby, but I had no idea it would be a big responsibility. I had so much anger stored up in me. That night in my cell I hauled off and smashed the metal headboard with my fist. They had to take me to the hospital. I sprained my entire hand.

I had mixed emotions in jail, who were the good guys and who were the bad guys. There were a few guards that were so nice, it was wonderful to see them come. One would play the guitar and we wrote songs. Wednesdays were general clean-up and we wrote a song about it. There were other guards who were harder to get along with.

When I got out of jail, my father came to pick me up. I had been a disappointment to my parents. My father told me that in the beginning when I got busted and my name was in the paper, he was worried about the family name. He told me that with God's help, he was able to work through that. He realized that regardless of what other people thought, I was his daughter.

During Dave's time of incarceration I wrote him a letter telling him I couldn't be one of his three girlfriends and that for mine and Jennifer's sake, he had to make a decision as to who he wanted to be with. I had fear in my heart that he wouldn't pick me. The response I got back was that he wanted to make a life with Jennifer and me. I was so happy. Three weeks after I got out, I went to see him. He was in Springhill Institution. My friend made the drive from Fredericton to Springhill with me, about four and a half hours. She didn't want me to go alone. When I came around the turn and saw Springhill, the thought of Dave locked up made me weep. It broke my heart to know he was there.

When he came into the visiting room it was ironic because he walked right past me. Let me explain. When I went to prison I weighed 82 pounds. I'm 5' 7" and the guard told me when she strip searched me, that I looked like a refugee that just came over on the boat. While in jail I gained approximately 50 lbs. Dave was the same. He had been working out on the weights in jail. It had been three months and I didn't recognize him either. We had become healthy. I continued to write and visit Dave. He made a commitment to Jesus in prison. I was still doing my thing on the street.

After his release, we got together again and things seemed okay to start. Then it got back to the same as before. The abuse started. Dave was a very angry and abusive man. I've worn army boots in my face and I've had my hair yanked out of my head. At times we'd be driving down the street and I would just be sitting there. Dave would start screaming at the top of his lungs. You never knew when he would just haul off and give you a smash in the face. There was a part of Dave, even through all of that, that I could see, that I felt no one else could see. I knew about his parents passing away and as we got closer, he would share more with me.

With our lifestyle, it was like we were living in two different worlds. We figured out one thing from our cocaine addiction, prior to incarceration, that we would never do it again. Dave never sold it and he had more control over it than I did. He could put it away at any given time but I couldn't stop. I wanted more and more.

Our relationship blossomed and on September 28, 1985, we got married. I had Meaghan the following year. We did okay for a while. Dave went into the hospital because he had a blood clot in his leg. He had an out-of-body experience and almost died. I thought he was dying. He had a private room in case he wanted to smoke marijuana. He went into the bathroom and smoked half a joint and came back to bed. Later on, he said he felt funny and told me to call the nurse. All of a sudden his eyes shot back in his head and he went into con-vulsions. I freaked and ran into the hall screaming for some-one to help. At one point, Dave had died and I can't begin to explain what happened to me, but terror gripped my heart. After the nurses got there, I had to go and sit in the corner. Jennifer was with me. She was three or four. He started say-ing "Jesus, Jesus". In my mind, because of my experience with him, I thought he was cursing, but in reality he was call-ing to Jesus. I found out later that he was coming back from the pits of hell. He came back because of calling out to Jesus.

Dave always had a connection to Christianity. When we were stoned on acid, which we did four or five nights a week with Rusty, they would start talking about the Bible. They spoke of the second coming and Christianity. I was doing drugs to get away from that stuff and they were doing drugs to find it. I would have a bad trip because of it. Dave always had a Bible. We would have cocaine parties in Harvey and he would sit and read the Bible for hours. In my mind, he was trying to figure out when the end was coming so he could get his foot in the door. I was hanging around because he was putting cocaine on the board. He wanted to read us the Bible. We wanted the coke.

After Dave's out-of-body experience, he didn't smoke dope for weeks. Then slowly, he got back into it and our life got worse. We'd stay up until 6 or 7 a.m. doing coke and I'd have to get up with the kids. In the midst of this, we were having kids. We are so blessed that our kids are normal because I was so stoned and abusive to my body even when I was pregnant. It is a miracle. Every Thursday was club house night. It was an-after hours bar and you could do anything there. They had pool tables and they served liquor. You could snort coke and smoke drugs. I looked forward to Thursdays to be around people.

One night, I had a girlfriend at the house. There were a couple of guys over that Dave was doing a deal with and Lori and I were downstairs in the bedroom doing cocaine. I was heavy into it and was stealing Dave's money. I was doing it behind his back when he was gone during the day. I would have other people deliver cocaine to me. They knew I was ripping him off. They were giving me garbage, cutting it, and goodness only knows what I was putting in my body.

Lori tells me I took about 1/4 gram up each nostril and went back on the bed into convulsions and stopped breathing. She didn't know what to do and Dave was out. Only the two guys were there. She screamed and the guys came in. One had to jump on my chest because I was turning blue. I came around and sat up on the bed and said, "Are you ready to go", and Lori burst into tears. One thing about overdosing on cocaine is that you don't know you're going under. Another time I had been on the phone and the kids found me. I was on the floor and I came to with the phone cord around my neck. The babysitter from next door was standing over me saying "Karen, if you don't stop this you're going to kill yourself". Jennifer and Meaghan were crying. I cannot imagine the devastation that it must have caused them.

Another time I OD'd in the bathroom and did what they call "the chicken". It is a seizure or type of convulsion. I cracked my head on the counter top. I was getting more and more involved in coke. It had such a grip on my life that I came to the place where I could not function or get out of bed without cocaine. I was totally and completely dependent.

I have a stepdaughter that I kept from time to time. She is eight months older than our oldest. She had been living near Toronto, Ontario, with her mother and boyfriend. We were to take care of her for the summer. At the end of August, we had planned on attending the Rolling Stones concert in Toronto. Dave had lots of money because of dealing. I also have a stepson who was 18 at that time and he was going with us. We rented a van. Dave, his son and daughter, me and our oldest daughter headed for Toronto. On the way there we happened to catch the Snowbirds plane crash on video.

On Sunday afternoon, we went to Niagara Falls and then back to the motel room for supper. We were sitting on the bed watching T.V. Dave felt a tremor behind him and looked back. I was going into convulsions. I was eight months and one week pregnant with our daughter and was in convulsions. Dave had no idea what was going on.

I sat up on the bed and was holding my head because I had always had terrible migraines, but this was not like them. I was rocking back and forth and said, "I can't see". He asked if I was blind and I said, "No, I just can't focus". The pain was so severe in my head that it was blurring my vision. Dave took me to the bathroom and splashed cold water on my face. He allowed me to lead him where I wanted to go. We ended up in the corridor and Dave told his son to call for help.

It was an emergency and I was very sick. I led him out by the elevators and began to vomit, then I slumped against the wall. Security and managers came and called 911. The ambulance came and took me to a Mississauga hospital where I was admitted.

They kept me sedated and I became conscious the next night, Monday, at suppertime. The nurse was in the room and she said something not nice to me like, "I bet you wish you'd stayed home". I went back to sleep and woke up on Tuesday. I had learned to lie well and could look you straight in the eye. The doctor came in and asked how I was. I lied and said "Fine, I want to go home". The vision had cleared but the pain in my head was awful. I was scared to death because I knew something was wrong. They released me on the condition that I would be taken to the doctor in Fredericton immediately.

We arrived back in Fredericton on Wednesday evening. The drive was awful. I couldn't eat, sleep, or smoke. We went straight to the hospital and they admitted me. They sedated me at about 11 p.m. and I came to at 5 a.m. I was in labour. It was the most difficult labour I had experienced, although it was the shortest. I was very scared. Lacie was delivered at 8 a.m. They thought everything was okay. People even came to visit me.

Dave came in on the third day to take me home. What I'm about to tell you isn't from my lips, because I don't have any recollection of the events. He came in and was talking to me. Then he went out and asked the nurse, "Who is that woman?" She told him that it was Mrs. Hardy and Dave said that it was not his wife. They called the doctor and they came and asked me who I was and did I know where I was. I couldn't answer. They moved me to the psychiatric ward. By the time they got me there, my body was all contorted, I was unable to walk or talk.

I took a turn for the worse on Friday. My family, especially my husband, went through a lot of emotional pain that I was unaware of because of my mental state. I went into a coma. My husband called out to God through a friend, Rusty Sullivan. He had been a drug friend, but had been saved. The doctors transferred me to the Saint John Regional Hospital neurological ward. They had no idea what had gone on.

Rusty says he came into my room and laid hands on me and prayed. He said he believed he touched heaven that night when he cried out to God on my behalf. Dave smoked a joint. Dave and Rusty followed the ambulance to Saint John. The doctors checked me over, and wanted to do some tests. As they drove home, Rusty's wife Mary, began to share with Dave and told him that she believed he was at a crossroads in his life. Dave had a choice to make and her belief was that if he didn't make the right choice, he may not have the chance again.

They left Dave at 2 a.m. and he knew that the 38 lbs of hash in the woods and the $50,000 - $100,000 he had from the drug scene made no difference. None of that could help him now. The only one who could help was God. He cried out to God. If God would heal his wife, not for his sake but for the sake of those four little girls; if He would send her home with a sound mind and body, then he would serve God for the rest of his life. Dave had three girls at home, one in the hospital and a wife on her deathbed. He left it with God and went to bed.

When I was transferred between hospitals, the word was out that the drug dealer's wife was very low, and a small group of Christians gathered to pray for me. One of the people we had done drugs with was with Dave in the mall. He pointed out Dan Sheridan and said he operates in healing. Dave wanted Dan to pray for me, even though he was a drug dealer. They went over and asked him to pray for me. They prayed right there in the mall, holding hands. At that exact time, there was a small prayer group who were also praying and interceding for me at Mike and Anne McLeans.

In the morning, Dave came to the hospital. They took him in one of those quiet rooms and told him they had done tests. They told him that from the drug abuse the blood vessels in my brain had shrunk so small that I had hemorrhaged on the frontal lobe on one side of my brain. Now I had the mind and body functions of a primitive child. I had no motor skills or control of my bowels or kidneys. He came to see me and I was in a diaper and tied to my bed. They didn't know if I would live or die. I had regressed to a very childlike state. For the next two weeks, Dave sat at my bedside, although I wasn't coherent. He was emotionally tormented. At that time he didn't use drugs. God's spirit came in and helped him through.

Most of the time I was unaware he was there for 12 or 14 hours a day. He did it every day, driving back and forth. On the fourteenth day they sent me to physiotherapy to see how far I had regressed. They planned to send me to a rehabilitation centre in Fredericton to try and train the other side of my brain to do the simple functions we take for granted: talking, walking, cooking and cleaning. They put me on a treadmill and I walked for 15 minutes. They sent me back and said there was nothing wrong with me.

That day, Dave came in and I was sitting up. I had to go to the bathroom so I got up and Dave almost fell out of his chair. He couldn't believe it. I hadn't even known what had gone on. He said, "Karen, you can walk!" I thought, of course I can, I'm 25 years old. He knew that the prayer that he had prayed that first night had been answered. A few days after that, with no medications, no operations, only observation, I walked out of the hospital, hand in hand with my husband, nineteen days after I went in. The doctors cannot explain it. God healed me completely.

Even though I had lived through it, I still wanted to use cocaine. That was the depth of the grip Satan had on me. Sunday morning I got up, we always sent our kids to Sunday school. This one day Dave was rummaging through the closet for clothes for church. I said, "We don't go to church" and he said " Today we do". We went to church and Dave cried through the whole service. I had never seen him cry. He had accepted Jesus into his life but it wasn't my thing. In his euphoria he thought I also had accepted Jesus. I had blocked that out.

We came home and life went on except we weren't using cocaine anymore. He was still dealing drugs and had to go pick up some money from a supplier who kept the best for us. When Dave came home, I was so angry that he didn't bring drugs home for us. He was so amazed. I became suicidal and told him that if I couldn't do coke anymore, I didn't want to live.

This was a crisis point in my life. I shared that with him and he came back and told our babysitter we were going for a drive to the gravel pit. My husband spouted out scripture that he didn't even know he knew and he led me to Jesus in the front seat of our car.

The feeling of freedom and peace was indescribable. Everything didn't change 100% at that moment but I knew that I had been forgiven for everything that I had done, including overdosing in front of my kids. I now knew that Jesus died for me. My spirit that had been dead in sin was awakened that night. It was the most important decision I had ever made. God didn't expect me to be perfect. He took a mess and made a message out of it.

The next 12 years of my life have been the most amazing time. I thought drugs, cops, and drug lifestyle was living on the edge, but there is nothing like living for Jesus to keep you on the edge. We never know what's around the corner.

After we dedicated our lives, it was the first time I had done something straight. I had been stoned my whole life. The simplest of tasks were all done stoned. We were stoned first thing in morning. To go from stoned to straight was all new to me. I remember the colours of nature became so much more vibrant, blue skies, green trees. Even the way I dressed changed and people commented. I had always worn black but now I wore colours. We didn't know what we were going to do. Part of the problem with coming clean was what to do. We had no job experience except drug dealing. Dave had some money put aside. We talked about dealing just until New Year's and if we put the money aside, we could make it. We both got our G.E.D. (Grade 12 equivalent) while in jail.

Dave went hunting one day and God spoke to him and told him to get off the fence and decide which way to go. He couldn't deal drugs and serve God. He came home and we decided to trust God to provide. Dave was concerned with telling people that he didn't want to deal anymore. We decided he would sell what he had left then he wouldn't buy anymore. It was difficult for other drug people to understand what Dave was going to do. He had to explain he was going to trust in God. A short while afterwards, an old friend came over to the house and told us the hash was better and cheaper. He was making more money and tried to get Dave back into it, but he stood strong.

It's been interesting. Dave totally immersed himself in the Word. He would go downstairs for 10 - 12 hours to read, while I cooked and looked after the kids. He didn't want to slip back since it had happened before and he almost lost it all. We did something every night. We did a Bible study or something else. There were Wednesday noon meetings with a chaplain. All of a sudden, we were aware of our children and the responsibility of raising them. We had kids 7, 3, 1 and a newborn. I remember our daughter, who was three at the time, having a temper tantrum in the bedroom. I called Dave at the chaplaincy because I didn't know what to do. It was a lot to do this straight and sober.

It was very important for Dave to be able to go to Andrew's on Wednesdays. It was the time for lots of people with our background to get together and pray. The few times I was able to go it was so positive. I remember the first Sunday we walked into Smythe Street Cathedral and heard Monty Lewis was going to be speaking. When Dave had his blood clot in the hospital and had his out-of-body experience, Monty had come in and offered Dave the opportunity to receive the Lord. We walked in wearing jeans and Harley shirts and barely off drugs. The church was so big and intimidating. People like us, feel very intimidated going into these places. There were three confirmations God gave us to let us know that this was the place for us.

There were home groups on Saturday night where we had Bible studies. These times were very important to us. We started with pot luck suppers where we could be ourselves and ask questions. It was the first place I prayed out loud. I was so nervous. They would have the guitar out and Dan Sheridan would play and sing. We did a study on the book of Romans in the Bible. As I read it over and over, it was new every time.

I wanted to find out why I had taken the path I did and why I had done the things I did. One of the big things to me, after 37 years, is the powerlessness that abuse created in my life as a child. Whether verbal, physical or sexual, I think Satan uses it to rob us of what God intends for our life. God uses my past, as in the story of Joseph, and takes what Satan meant for bad, and uses it for good in my life and the lives of others.

I believe we must be open and honest. Transparency is the key. I have to be a transparent individual because if I'm not, I am being phony. The enemy will tell us lies about ourselves. We'll think we are the only ones experiencing this and everyone will think we're weird or terrible. We take on all these thoughts, behaviours and attitudes when they are not us at all. Satan is a liar and he has stolen from us.

God has brought me through several stages of the healing process. He showed me several years ago that "deeper is darker" and there are different levels to healing. This is important because those are the words that the Lord gave me. They have made a great impact not only on myself but with other women I work with. God wants to go to the root but there are little arms and feelers along the way and so many things that need to be healed. The deeper He goes in the healing process, the darker and uglier it seems to become. In each step of healing I have received God's grace and mercy making me stronger for the next step.

Dave and I both went back to university. Dave completed his degree in four years. I took five years to finish because I took an extra major. Dave graduated with honours in Sociology and a minor in Psychology. I graduated with a major, with honours, in Sociology, a double major in Criminology and a minor in Psychology and Religious Studies. It was difficult but it was a time for discipline.

We shared our testimony in sociology class and the professor was amazed we even had brains to function with. There were lots of struggles in University. We didn't even know what plagiarism was. We set goals and we achieved them. God was with us. He taught me to embrace adversity to strengthen me.

I didn't want to get an education at the expense of my children. They were just little at the time. Fortunately we were able to arrange our schedules so that most of the time I was gone, the children were napping or at school. It all flowed together. Yes, it was stressful and hard. The only time I had to study was in the evenings when the children were in bed. I needed quiet and structure to concentrate.

We went from living on a drug dealer's salary to living

on a $864 welfare cheque for the month. We'd had no discipline in our lives. God has been molding us and shaping us over the last twelve years to show others what He can do. The fact that we graduated from University is a miracle in itself.

We always enjoyed riding motorcycles. God has enabled us to become part of a Christian motorcycle chapter. There was one that was initiated by my husband and another gentlemen and it was called Kingdom Riders. We were with that for quite some time. I was able to wear colours. I had "Jesus is Lord" and "Born Again" on my back. It was a whole new experience.

We then became members of CMA (Christian Motorcyclists Association) and they have over 50,000 members world-wide. I am the secretary for our motorcycle chapter. We go to secular bike runs and just show how we live. Jesus also gave me the strength to get my own motorcycle license. We have a good time and we don't have to do drugs and alcohol anymore. People can see the peace and joy that Jesus has brought to our lives.

We have four beautiful daughters who are all serving Jesus. God has a plan for all our lives. He took me from being a stoned-out druggie to a stand-up woman in my community and an example to my children.

God has worked and is still working in areas of my life. I remember going to the Twelve Step Overcomer's Group at the church, especially for females. I didn't want to fake it anymore; I wanted to be real. I had played games for so long, I was tired of it. I thought if I told everybody that I didn't work sexually, they would think I was odd or weird, or that there was something wrong with me. Funny how Satan will take negative things in our lives, that we don't bring on ourselves, and twist them to make us think there is something wrong with us. I think that is part of the deceptive nature of the enemy. He takes things God created to be good and twists them, just as he did in the Garden when he twisted the truth.

I was in emotional and spiritual agony at the group. I wanted to reveal the whole thing because I was tired of having feelings of guilt, shame and feeling dirty. I couldn't explain the thoughts in my head. I thought, "God if I tell these people, they are going to think I'm terrible". The enemy had twisted my mind.

I tried to telephone my friend, about fifty times to tell her about it. I knew that in order to be set free, I had to bring this to the light. I didn't know if I could be set free but I had faith in God. I truly believed that if I released it, that God would do something in me. I was tired of playing games and being phony in my sex life with my husband. I finally got the courage to tell her over the phone. The conversation she had with me, blew me away. Not only had she experienced the same thing, but she had worked through it with Jesus her husband and had gained victory. This gave me hope. I don't know to this day if she knows how much hope that gave me.

So I began the journey back in the Twelve Step group for women. I thought, "Lord, tonight I am going to share this", and so many times I went there with that in my heart, but I never had the courage. This night, it must have been the power of the Holy Spirit, but God allowed me to release it and when I spoke it out, fear gripped my heart just for an instant. I know that 85% of the women in that group had experienced similar, if not equal or worse situations, and they were also suffering. God used me to share my own darkness and that, in turn, allowed others to share theirs. I found out that night that I wasn't alone, or the only one faking sex.

Many women suffer from the same thing. God taught me something that night. No matter how bad I was, or what I'd done, or what had been done to me, there is someone else suffering from the same thing. I praise God that He brought me to the place where I could share this problem. Many women have been set free as I have shared my experiences of sexual abuse and healing with them.

I shared it with my friend and now the group, but the next step was to share it with my husband. This was the most difficult thing I have ever had to do. Although I believed in my husband and we loved each other, there was still fear and intimidation in me about sharing that with him because I had been lying to him all those years.

Again I went through the emotional struggle of wanting to tell him and not being able do it. Then one night God gave me the strength to tell Dave that I had been faking my emotions and responses in my sex life all those years. Again Satan came in and twisted it around. He attacked my husband and his manhood. Dave got upset with me. His initial reaction was that I wasn't the woman he married. I was finally able to help him see that it wasn't his fault. As a result of all the sexual abuse I had endured from the ages of three to nine, my body had physically shut down in the response mode. I couldn't respond normally, in a sexual way with my husband. We cried, prayed, laughed, and talked. It took a lot of work, but eventually God released me and my husband and brought us to the place where we now enjoy a normal sexual relationship.

I have been able to get involved in women's chaplaincy and in the prisons. I use the Overcomer's Twelve Step Group. It has helped many to know freedom inside ourselves, enabling us to share with others the same principles found in God's Word. Even in the writing of this story for this book, God has been setting me free, as I have worked through different events in my life.

Now that I have the experienced forgiveness and grace in my life, no-one could tell me that Jesus isn't real. I'm not perfect but God has done so much in my life. David Mainse of 100 Huntley Street asked Dave and I to share our story on the program. We couldn't believe we were even being asked. We've had the opportunity to do the 700 Club as well. I'm not trying to glorify myself, I just want to show other women that "who the Son sets free is free indeed". It's not about rules or membership in a certain denomination, it is simply about a relationship with Jesus. Even though I was lost in sin, He was able to restore me. He can restore anyone who submits to Him.

Karen Hardy
c/o the Saint John Community Chaplaincy
36 Sewell St.
Saint John, New Brunswick
E2L 3A2

Bob – Collin's Bay Penitentiary, 1982

Top 10 Most Wanted in Canada

The Life
of
ROB McGRATH

My co-accused and I were handcuffed together in the back of a squad car and were being transported to Cobourg, then on to the Federal Penitentiary in Kingston, Ontario. As we sat in the back of the cruiser, I was able to take the handcuffs off. When we stopped in front of the next county jail, we stepped out of the cruiser carefully. I booted the car door and this shook the police officer who fell to the ground. I took off. There was a major police hunt with police dogs. This was serious business for the small town of Cobourg. I was now on the run.

Prison was a way of life for our family. There were seven children in all. I was born on March 5, 1958. I remember growing up in a dysfunctional family and some of the problems, storms and issues that were ongoing in our home among family members. I remember fist fights and brawls going on continually. I remember cases of beer and wine coming into the house. There were marijuana plants growing in the windows. At the age of seven or eight, I was desperately looking for love; for someone to embrace me and someone to encourage me. Unfortunately there was a lot of drunkenness, instability, confusion, anger and rage in the hearts of my family members, so love was in short supply.

My father used to come home from the bars at all hours of the night drunk, angry and confused. My mother and he slept in separate rooms in the house. He used to force me to come into his room and sit on the floor. Then he would drink whiskey while chain smoking and verbally abuse me. He told me I was an idiot, a loser and I'd never amount to anything and I'd probably spend my life in prison. If I started to fall asleep, he would slap me in the face and kick me. At such a young age this was difficult for me to deal with. I was very angry and confused. I had a lot of mixed feelings and emotions in my heart. Anger bottled up inside me towards my father and others.

I prayed to Jesus many times. I didn't know Him, but I believed Jesus died on the cross for my sins. My family were Irish Catholics, and there was an acknowledgement of a God or Higher Power, but no-one was committed to Jesus Christ. When I was young I went to Sunday School, so I was exposed to the things of the Bible. Sadly, no-one ever took a special interest in me to help me. I struggled with a sense of identity and purpose in life. I never had a decent role model to reinforce good morals and standards.

At home, my younger sister and I leaned on each other for comfort. We used to sit at the top of the stairs at night crying and watching the fighting that was always going on. Fist fights were common place between our father, mother, brothers and even some visitors who came to our house. There was always plenty of beer and lots of whiskey and wine. The brawls would go on for hours at a time. Sometimes people would be knocked to the floor and kicked unconscious. One night during a fight, dad was knocked unconscious. He fell and lost a lot of blood. Then the dog came and licked up all the blood. We saw furniture being smashed. I remember bottles flying through the air and my sister and I were always

108

terrified. There were many situations where people were beaten half to death.

One time my father hit my brother with a two by four and broke his jaw. Another time he went to drop a large brick on my other brother while he was sleeping. I yelled out, "Johnny" and thank goodness he moved or he would have been dead. My father beat us with all kinds of different objects like plastic baseball bats. He thought nothing of using his belt and the buckle on our backs, heads and faces. If we ever came in later than our curfew, he would wait in the darkened kitchen and when we came in, he would cut loose like a wild animal. I had been smashed in the face several times, booted, kicked, knocked down and kicked across the floor like a dog. One time he hit my head with such force, I flew across the room, hit the fridge and the door caved in. It was an old fridge and they were built pretty strong.

One day mom made a nice meal and it really looked good. We were all sitting around the supper table. I had been lippy with mom that morning and my father looked at me and said, "So you'd rather be in Training School, eh?". I hung my head sheepishly, filled with fear. My father had been a boxer in the army so he was really strong. He came up out of his chair and drove me straight in the face with his fist and continued to pound me. He was like a wild man. The table went flying and there was food and blood everywhere. The power of his blow sent me into the shed door. My mother jumped in to try to save me but my father had terrorized the whole family. I vowed that one day I would kill my father. I was very bitter and angry.

Between the ages of six and seven I was placed in a foster home because my parents were in prison for possession of stolen goods. I'd really work hard for the farmers where I was placed. I remember sitting at the end of the long laneway with the old farm dog waiting for my father to come and get me. But he never did come. I was a lonely, insecure little boy who desperately needed to be loved.

At home, alcohol consumed most of the money we had for food. We often ate cereal that was found in the dump or the garbage. Many times we ate it with water not milk. One time, my sister and I went to the fridge and the only thing in there was a pound of butter. We sat and ate it with two spoons. It sure tasted good, but we got really sick afterwards. Clothing was another issue. The first one up in the morning was the best dressed for the day. On my feet I used to wear bread bags for socks.

I liked to stay over at my friends' houses (the few friends I had) because I'd have a clean bed and a nice meal. One Christian family had me over and they hugged me and showed me a measure of love. They invited me to Sunday School several times and I was happy to go. I wore my cleanest dirty clothes. At Sunday School, the other kids laughed at me and called me "a slum" and other names because I wore those rags to church. I just didn't fit in. I couldn't even make it in Sunday School. I was a nobody, just like my Dad said. It was coming true.

My father and I never had a healthy relationship, so I drifted into all kinds of trouble. I even got involved in criminal activities with my brothers. When I was nine years old, I was molested by someone close to the family. This compounded the problems and created an intense rage in me.

When I was 10 years old, I was well acquainted with alcohol. My oldest brother gave me a bottle of whiskey and I drank that down. That opened up the door for more major problems. My father gave me alcohol and I was well on my way to becoming a big-time loser. By the time I was 12 years old, I had been in and out of Juvenile Courts many times for a variety of criminal activities. I'd been stealing cars and breaking and entering homes and businesses. There were fist fights on the street and the police were continually picking me up. One time I was sitting in a railroad box car and drinking. All of a sudden I started to cry. I was struggling with so many mixed feelings and one of my friends said, "What are you crying for?" I told him that no-one loved me and he hauled off and gave me a smash in the face to smarten me up.

I remember my father taking me to National Grocers and other places to steal for him. I stole cigarettes, food items and lots of other things. He also encouraged other family members to steal to provide for him accordingly. I guess this is where I got the idea that stealing and criminal behaviour was okay, as long as you didn't get caught, and you were willing to share the dividends with others. My father used to say to me, "If you're going to be a thief, be a good one. Go to the

110

banks because that's where the money is". My other brothers robbed and stole continually and both parents capitalized on our behaviour.

The home situation continued to be stormy. It wasn't unusual to see people being taken out in leg irons, cuffs and straight jackets. Windows got kicked out. Doors were kicked off their hinges. There was destruction everywhere. It was a hellish environment to grow up in. At 10 or 11 years of age I was a very unstable individual. I was using drugs and I felt unloved, uncared for and rejected. I felt I had been cut off from any type of love, affection and acceptance, even from my own family. This only compounded the anger towards my father. At 11 I wanted to be a gangster, to carry a gun and rob people. I just wanted to lash out and take what I wanted.

Because of the family name, McGrath, our reputation and our criminally-inclined behaviours, the neighbours didn't want their children to associate with us. That in turn created more hatred and anger in me. At school I had a lot of problems. I was a slow learner and I found it difficult to concentrate. It was suggested that I be sent to a special school for disadvantaged or handicapped children. The other kids would tease me and mouth off about my family. Even here, rejection was a big part of my life. Many times I was given the strap for fighting. One teacher, Eric Sloan, took a special interest in me and took me on as kind of a special project. He played a very important part in my life. With his help, I was able to gain some ground and pass some grades.

By the time I was 12 years old, I had a real chip on my shoulder. I was continually engaging in alcohol abuse and interacting with other criminals. I was carrying a gun, a 38 Smith and Wesson. I smoked pot and injected speed into my arms. I was also experimenting with acid. I didn't like myself. I was very insecure and angry and I was lashing out at society. Life was a real problem for me.

I was well on my way to becoming a career criminal. I was in the criminal subculture. I was interested in the Satan's Choice motorcycle gang. They were my heroes and role models. Many of the members were close to my family, especially my brothers. One of the club houses was just down the street from where we lived. I really liked that lifestyle and felt it was for me.

One night my brother and I went to a farmhouse to deal with an individual who had punched my mother in the face and blackened her eyes. I had a 10 inch butcher knife down the back of my pants. As we arrived, my brother asked me to see if I could find a club. I found a baseball bat and gave it to him. We burst in. There was a poker game going on with lots of drinking and partying. We let out a roar and told the individual that we were there to teach him a lesson he would never forget.

Within a couple of minutes the guy went down on the floor with a baseball bat to the head. He went into a coma, caught pneumonia and died. My brother was charged with non-capital murder. I guess I should have been charged also, but I was sent to Reform School for rebellious boys.

It was a Catholic Training School and there were a lot of difficulties there. I remember being physically beaten, punched, and sexually abused. Since it was a Catholic Training School, there were religious rituals and a belief system of God and Jesus Christ. I believed in Jesus and I prayed at night to a Jesus I didn't know. I became an altar boy and I was looking to Jesus in a half hearted way. My heart was very calloused by now and the abuse in the school compounded it.

I was angry and rebellious and often lashed out at others, including the staff. I ran away many times, only to get into more trouble with the law. I broke into homes and businesses and stole cars. I didn't care if I lived or died. Inside was a broken little boy who wanted to break away from the lifestyle, but didn't have the skills or the encouragement needed to do this.

I spent approximately four years in the training school and when I was released at 16 I was an accident looking for a place to happen. I was released into Peterborough, Ontario and I landed a job working in a carpentry factory. There was lots of potential, but with my problems, it didn't last very long.

I met a young lady who was living at home with her grandparents. They were very special and unique people. We hooked up and cultivated a relationship which was very co-dependent. We were like the blind leading the blind. She played a very special part in my life. We began living together and planned someday to marry and have a family. Because

112

of alcohol and being outside of God's will, and with all the different problems and issues we were struggling with, the relationship ended.

Six to eight months after I was released from the farm school system, I had many major encounters with the law for a variety of criminal activities. I was charged with assault causing bodily harm and attempted robbery on a motel and some other things. I was 16 and a half and I was sentenced to two years less a day with four and a half years concurrent. I was sent into the Provincial Reformatory System.

I went to Brantford Correctional Institution, which was kind of lenient considering my background. I got a job working in the kitchen and got involved with my biker role models again. I was continually trying to prove something; that I was somebody. There were several violent confrontations and the prison officials were concerned about my instability and violent behaviour. For the good of the institution it was decided that I should be sent to a maximum security lock-down situation or institution. I was sent to Millbrook.

After I heard that this was where I was heading, I organized an escape with another man from the U.S. We got away and I was unlawfully at large. It wasn't too long before I found myself being chased by the police because I was in a stolen vehicle. I had broken into a business and after a high-speed chase, I was taken into custody and taken to the Provincial Court in Cobourg. I was given an additional 15 months on top of the two years less a day, and I was sent to Kingston Federal Penitentiary. I was only 17 years old and I was being sent to one of the oldest and toughest prisons in Canada.

When they slammed those doors shut behind me in Kingston, fear gripped my heart. I was in a place I really didn't want to be. The name MacGrath was well known in the prison system. I had three brothers in prison. One was at Collins Bay, one was in Joyceville and one in Warkworth Penitentiary. This created other difficulties for me, such as living up to the family name. I found myself continually having problems with the prison staff. Fist fights and brawls were a common way of life for me in prison. Many times I was locked in solitary confinement, being placed in cells in locked-down situations.

Things got worse and my heart got more calloused. I served 30 months on this sentence and was released in 1977. I then went to live in Kingston, Ontario. I got a job in an autobody repair shop. I had all kinds of potential and the bosses took a liking to me. I was a very willing and capable worker, but alcohol and drugs still played a big part in my life. I went bar hopping and got caught up in the criminal subculture again.

One night, when I was full of alcohol and drugs, I took a shotgun and robbed the Holiday Inn in Kingston. I really believe if it wasn't for the mercy and grace of God that night I would have lost my life. There was a police officer who pulled his revolver out and yelled, "Halt or I'll shoot". I turned to him and told him to go ahead and shoot. He fired one shot and I kept going. He fired a second shot and if not for the grace of God I would be dead.

I was involved with a woman at that time who was involved in the occult. She was into tarot cards, crystal balls and palm reading. She was messed up big time. After that robbery, I was sent back to the penitentiary with another four years to do. Once again I found myself involved in all kinds of problems in the institution. There were fist fights, brawls, power struggles and smash ups.

I got involved with the bikers once again. One individual in particular, called the Sergeant of Arms and I got along really well. We looked out for each other for protection. Around this time I got involved with Martial Arts, Body Building and Boxing. I found myself driven to get into shape. I was driven by a dark force and by hate. I was a danger to others and myself. I was on a real power trip. If anyone got in my way, I could kill them in a second, it really didn't matter.

I transferred to another institution where I met a wealthy drug manufacturer who was just passing through the system. We became good friends. He said, "I've been looking for one good man and if you're willing to work for me, I'll give you anything you want". It was a pretty impressive proposition to a 21 year old. This very wealthy Greek drug manufacturer hired me as his personal body guard and my job was to protect him.

I was released from prison on day parole shortly after I met this person. On day parole I met other criminals who

114

were caught up in the fast lane. I carried a gun and wore three piece suits. I had a Harley-Davidson, a T-bird and a duplex house. Satan was grooming me and giving me everything I had ever wanted. I was involved in drug deals, high-speed chases and all kinds of criminal activity. Many times my life, or someone else's life, could have been taken.

After some small time drug dealers were robbed of various quantities of drugs and cash, several of my co-accused were picked up by the local police. After going through the investigation, three of them made deals with the police to get lighter sentences. Shortly after that, I was picked up. The police told me I was in the Big Leagues now. I laughed at them and told them to get off my case. I was then sentenced to seven years, consecutive to the previous sentence, which landed me nine years in the Federal Penitentiary.

My co-accused and I were handcuffed together in the back of a squad car. The men in the cruiser transporting us to the Penitentiary in Kingston were RCMP (Royal Canadian Mounted Police) officers. One had been on the force for 23 years and was about to retire. When I escaped, I knew he would have liked to corner me himself. They put me on the Top 10 Most Wanted list in Canada. I was considered armed and dangerous because in some of the robberies I had committed, shots were fired. My life was now on the line.

I was on the run for about 10 days. I hooked up with some old buddies and after doing some cocaine and partying, I was told I could go anywhere in the world with a new identity if I'd come back once in a while to do someone a favour. After weighing the pros and cons, I figured if I ran somewhere there would be an another encounter with the law. There undoubtedly would be gun play and someone could lose their life. It could just as easily be me.

In 1980 I made a decision and now I know that the Lord was in it. At that time I had nine and a half years to serve in the Federal Penitentiary. I secured a lawyer and made arrangements to turn myself in to the local police in Niagara Falls. The police were shocked at the turn of events. Nobody just walked in and surrendered when they were looking at that much time and probably having more added to their sentence.

I was transported back to Cobourg and given an additional 15 months and was on my way back to Collins Bay Penitentiary. I can honestly say that, from 1980 on I had a good taste of hell right here on earth. For the first two years, I was filled with a terrible depression. It got so bad that I contemplated suicide. I was caught up in all kinds of violence in prison. There were attempts on my life and one in particular was especially vicious. Someone cut my throat with a straight razor so that my neck was slashed open. God was obviously with me, because it missed my jugular vein. Had that vein been cut, I would have bled to death.

When I went to shower I wore shorts and work boots. I had a piece of steel hidden under my towel because I never knew when someone would come at me and try to kill me. I've been stabbed several times. I've been stabbed in the back, head and shoulder and I've stabbed others. I'm not very proud of these things. The things I saw and experienced must have come straight from Satan and the pit of hell.

I flirted with the Bible as I had them around me. I was involved with chapel service. I had crosses around my neck because I believed in Jesus Christ, God the Father and the Holy Spirit. I had all the outward signs, but there was nothing inside. I spent seven years, from 1980 to 1987 inside the Federal system. Life was very difficult. There were times I wanted to commit suicide because I couldn't see any kind of a future ahead for me.

While in prison, I went back to school at 22 years of age. I started at a Grade 4 level and finished Grade 11. I got involved in child psychology, child psychiatry, drug programs and Alcoholics Anonymous. I became the secretary-chairman of those groups. I was involved in lots of physical fitness programs, like boxing and working out, but I was still a ship without a port.

I also got involved with various religious belief systems. I flirted with Eastern religion, astral travel and satanism. I was reading stuff by Anton Le Vey, the head of the Satanic church in the US. I was reading the Satanic Bible and passing it around to other bikers and criminals. Satan was truly ruling my life. I recall a song by Bob Dylan that said, "You gotta serve somebody. It may be the devil or it may be the Lord, but you gotta serve somebody". I didn't realize that I

116

was serving Satan. I was messed up big time. I had tattoos all over my body, on my chest and arms, and I even had the name Lucifer written on my cell door.

There was something deep inside of me that wanted to settle down and live a good life, work at my own business and break away from the criminal scene and lifestyle. I know that desire was placed there by God. During this time I was tremendously uplifted by letters from Ernie Hollands who loved and encouraged me.

I was released in 1987 and I was like Humpty Dumpty on the inside. I smiled and gave the impression that I had it all together but I didn't. I hit the street and got right back into alcohol and the criminal subculture. I was on the street for 30 days, robbing and stealing and other activities, when the Winnipeg police took me into custody. I was taken back to Ontario where I received another 15 months on top of the previous sentence.

I was taken to Millhaven Penitentiary in 1987. While I was there I started reading testimony books of people who had given their lives to Jesus. I got hold of a book by C.S. Lovett called "Dealing With The Devil". I was locked up for 23 hours a day so I had lots of time to read. At that time I was 30 years old and had served 14 years in the prison system. I came to the realization from the Holy Spirit that I was indeed serving Satan. I realized who I was at that point and cried out to Jesus Christ to have mercy on a guy like me. At this point I realized that the devil was trying to kill me and take my soul to hell.

Jesus came into my life. He set me free on the inside. He put a song in my heart. He put a smile on my face. He put peace in my heart. He gave me a hunger and thirst to know Him and serve Him. I bought a Bible off a jailhouse merchant for two cartons of cigarettes. They'll sell you anything in there. I bought a big King James Bible and I studied the Word of God for hours on end. I fasted and prayed all the time. God had a wonderful plan and purpose for my life. I was able to share my faith and hope with others about my new life in Jesus. God gave me tremendous opportunities to witness to many individuals and lead others to Christ.

During this time I contacted other Christians in the community including Ernie and Sheila Hollands. They encouraged me tremendously and helped me grow. Many other Christians also ministered to me.

When I was released in January 1989, I left with a lot of deep rooted problems and issues that needed to be sorted out. It had been a challenging road to travel. I got involved with a local Bible believing church but I felt somewhat rejected. I felt alienated and isolated. One individual found out that I was an ex-convict. As word got around, people began to distance themselves from me in various ways and I picked up on that. I struggled with that and questioned whether I belonged in this church or setting. I did have expectations that I placed on these people but they didn't live up to them. It was a very difficult transition from the prison to the local church. Being unskilled in communications and coping skills, I had to face a lot of hurdles.

One day as I was struggling with these circumstances, the Holy Spirit spoke to me. He told me to take the initiative, go the extra mile and reach out with kindness and consideration. I did this and it wasn't long before I saw the miracle working power of Jesus. Others started to become more open towards me. Lines of communication opened. People started warming up to me and that helped a lot. I was able to cope with the challenges that came my way.

I was not lazy in prison, I worked in the machine shop, the carpenters' shop, autobody shop, the sheet metal shop and the food services department. I also worked in the butcher shop and received a retail meat cutting license so I had lots of saleable skills. There was no luck in the job department even with these.

Ernie and Sheila put me in touch with John Howson. He worked with 100 Huntley Street, a T.V. program in Winnipeg. He referred me to the personnel department of a carpentry factory in Winnipeg. I got the job. I worked long, hard hours and was blessed in my job. I received raises and was able to start saving money.

I was also able to go out on the streets and minister to those who were sleeping in the gutters, people in detox centres, soup kitchens, missions and anywhere people were struggling. I was able to share the love and the hope of the Lord Jesus Christ.

I joined the Waves of Glory Full Gospel Church and

Pastor Wieb and Gerry Lecture took me on. They loved me, rebuked me and helped me fine tune my faith and thinking. Later I began ushering at the church and three to four months after that, I became Head Usher with all the responsibilities that it entailed.

One day I was watching a slide presentation and listening to an East Indian lady named Kamlesh sharing about her latest trip to India. She was talking about the needs in this third world country. As she shared her heart about the poverty, sickness and disease, my heart was touched by the Holy Spirit. I could identify with the needs that were portrayed. Coincidentally, I had done a study on Calcutta while I was in prison. I said, "Lord that's the kind of woman I need in my life. Someone who is totally committed to you". I prayed a half-hearted prayer and asked the Lord that if it was His will, that that woman would be my wife.

I left this in God's hands. I never pursued her or went looking for a relationship. I believe God has a perfect mate for us. One day as I came out of a store, Kamlesh came out of nowhere. We started to talk and went to church together. After one year as friends, a relationship of love formed. We were both being cautious not to go against the will of the Lord. We fasted and prayed and God confirmed that it was His will that we were to be married, and we could serve Him as a team.

Kamlesh was born in Delhi, India. She was raised in the Indian tradition and at 19, her parents arranged a marriage for her with a Sikh in Uganda, Africa. She had three children, a son and two daughters. After 18 years she was left alone and decided to start a new life in Britain with her children. Eventually she came to Canada and became a hair stylist in Winnipeg. In 1983, Kamlesh accepted Jesus Christ as her Lord and Saviour and was born again. In serving the Lord she has been back to India to minister to those on the streets, hotels and anywhere needy people were to be found.

The Lord was gracious to me in giving me a beautiful wife who was 100% committed to Jesus and to me, her husband. Before we were married, I was able to buy a two bedroom bungalow. Eventually, I opened an autobody shop. Kam and I often took people into our house who were in need. We let them stay in our spare room and the Lord blessed us further.

When Kamlesh and I were married, we went to visit Vancouver. While we were there, we saw people struggling desperately. We thought to ourselves that this would be a wonderful mission field. After a few days we went home and fasted and prayed. The Lord confirmed His will. We rented out our home, gave away most of our belongings and launched out ,by faith, to serve the Lord in a new way.

We came to Vancouver and shortly after arriving there, I met a man named Paul who had fallen away from serving the Lord, and I took him out for breakfast. He had spent the night on the steps of a church. He was struggling with narcotics and alcohol. I told him he was living in sin and I asked him if he wanted to deal with his issues. We prayed together and Paul rededicated his life to Jesus and he was set free.

He told me about a local drop-in centre or mission where he had been a few days earlier and I went over there. It was an old bar that had been converted to the Union Gospel Mission. It was filled with street people. I told the director about myself and he was excited about my testimony. He encouraged me to get involved there. Several weeks later, while I was volunteering, I started to see people accepting Jesus Christ. After about 60 - 90 days as a volunteer I was taken to meet the president, Morris McAray. Morris hired me as the Assistant Director. After a few months, the Acting Director left and I took over his position.

While I was at the Centre during the day, Kamlesh would go to the streets of Vancouver to share God's love. By wearing her traditional dress, she has been able to minister to many of her own people and see them find peace through faith in Jesus.

I approached the board and asked if my wife could work with me in the food service department, and to minister to the ladies. Kam was given the job. The Lord brought a special young man into our lives, Troy Galardi, who joined the team.

For seven years, we ran the mission working with street people, drug addicts, alcoholics and others struggling with life crises. We moved into a small apartment at the back of the facility. It was an awesome ministry. We saw hundreds have their lives changed by the power of Jesus as Lord and

Saviour. Kam and I became like mom and dad to all those broken souls who came through our door. It was exciting!

We watched as some of these same people who made commitments to the Lord, leave and go and live in hotel rooms and places were there were lots of drugs and alcohol. Many precious souls drifted back into sin. We worked hard over the years trying to change these situations. Over the years, the Lord gave me a desire to open up a home for certain individuals who had made commitments to the Lord. I drafted up a submission and presented it to the Board. The proposal was turned down.

A year later, three or four people who were involved with me, felt that we should step out and open up a home and start discipling new Christians. The Lord provided all the tools and resources to make the initial step of faith. We secured a four bedroom home in Burnaby and furnished it. We worked with five or six men at the time and it was an extended family living arrangement. It was called The House of the Good Shepherd. There were amazing results. The program included Bible study, fellowship, worship, and prayer. We began attending Full Gospel Business Mens Fellowship, local churches and various types of outreach as a family.

Yes, there was lots of stress and pressure. There was lots of opposition from others who were not in favour of this project. We persevered and eventually opened up three more homes. At one point, we even had a home for women. I was carrying two jobs, as the Director of the Union Gospel Mission and Drop-In Centre and the House of the Good Shepherd Home. Today, we have a three floor facility where we work with people struggling with life threatening problems and addictions. We have a counseling training centre and administration offices in Burnaby, B.C.

I recall one particular brother who came to live in our home. He had come from a violent background filled with drugs. He made a commitment to the Lord and came to live in one of our other homes for quite a long time. He even brought his little boy to live with him there. We saw wonderful changes in Mike's life. Today he is a licensed drug and alcohol counselor and has a job working for Social and Family Services in Vancouver. His is a genuine success story

Bob, Kamlesh, Troy Garlardi – Vice President -
House of Good Shepherd Ministries

all due to the grace of God and caring Christians who invest-
ed in him.

After seven years we left the Union Gospel Mission.
There were many challenges to overcome. Launching out
into a full time ministry, we were faced with establishing a
financial engine to pull the train, so to speak. We also needed to facilitate and delegate the work and responsibilities to
keep things focused in the area of outreach. We've had to
generate support and deal with the media for interviews. It
has been very challenging to say the least. But God's grace
and wisdom have always been there and seen us through, and
continues to do so.

The Lord has opened doors in prisons where we visit
Federal, Provincial and Young Offenders facilities. In the
youth facilities, we have made great headway with the young
boys and teenagers. Many have made commitments to Jesus.
The challenge is to assist them when they are released, disciple them and help them make the transition to a local church.

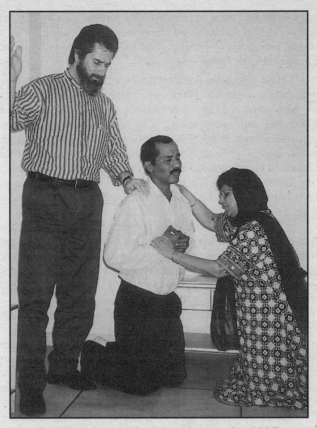

Bob and Kamlesh in Bombay, India 1997

The Lord has enabled my lovely wife and I to travel to India. Kamlesh speaks five languages so we are able to minister in many places there. Through the Holy Spirit we have been able to see great and mighty things happen as we travel through the slums of India. We've seen many souls come to Christ. We have established a basement flat in Delhi and it is kept for missionary outreach work.

We are grateful to God for our bus ministry. We go out into the streets and hard places where people are strung out on drugs and such. Many are homeless people and our ministry believes "from our seats to the streets". Every day we see wonderful results as we travel around, providing for their needs, giving them clothing, food and a message of hope and change through Jesus.

I have also been privileged to speak on different television programs such as 100 Huntley Street; It's a New Day out of Manitoba; the Bernice Gerrard program from British Columbia and many others. I've shared my testimony at camp meetings, at schools, to police officers, and to correctional staff. I've been blessed to receive a pardon from the Canadian Government. I have no criminal record today and I am able to cross the borders. I've also been privileged to go to Bible School, and have been licensed as an ordained minister.

It has not been an easy road to get where I am today. I've had to deal with a lot of inward conflicts, anger, bitterness, hatred, and unforgiveness. I've had to grow to trust and appreciate other people. In many ways I've had to deal with issues that many others may not have to because of the fact that I spent over half my life locked up in institutions.

I thank the Lord for what He is doing in the lives of my family members. I have been privileged to pray with each of my brothers. Four of them that are still alive and one has passed on. One of my sisters has passed on and so have my parents. Though all four of my brothers have said yes to Jesus, to date they have not made him Lord of their lives. But I know God is working on them even now.

My sister Liz has given her life to Jesus and is serving Him faithfully and growing in her faith. She is blessing many others and I am so grateful to the Lord .

My mother drank and smoked herself to death in 1980. She was a young woman of 49 years. Satan snuffed her out. My father had just turned 62, when he died. He was a whiskey drinker and chain smoker. On his deathbed he looked up into the faces of my younger sister and brother and with a cry said, "This is a hard way to go". Then he slipped on into eternity. I don't know where my parents stood with Jesus.

My other sister, was 26 years old and a beautiful woman. She had two teenage boys and a newborn baby. She got

Bob – President, House of Good Shepherd
Counselling Centre Vancouver, BC

hooked on pharmaceutical drugs and alcohol. One day, down
at the river bank, she dove in the water. She drowned that day.
My brother John spent many years in prison. When I was
waiting to visit him in the hospital with an escort, I got word
that he was in a coma. He had broken bones in his body and
was found on the lawn. We don't know how he ended up that
way. He was only 34 years old, but I know that he had made
a commitment to the Lord Jesus Christ just prior to his death.

I was considered a four time loser and a habitual criminal. I remember a Crown Attorney in Peterborough, Ontario saying, "he'll never change. He'll spend the rest of his life in prison. He's just like his brothers". Yes, one of them did 18 years in prison, another about 8 1/2 years, one did about 6 and one did about 3 years. Both my parents did time in prison, as did my sister that passed away. The world couldn't change me. Programs couldn't change me. Secular psychology and psychiatry couldn't change me. Only the power of Jesus could change me.

I have received so many blessings and miracles in my life, but by far, the greatest miracle was the gift of salvation, receiving Jesus Christ into my heart in 1987. I was lost, broken, depressed and confused but Jesus came into my heart and set me free. He healed my broken heart. Finally I found the love and acceptance I craved all my life in the love of Jesus. He can do the same for you. You can come just as you are. He will save you, heal you and love you.

You know, I'm not just happy because I now have a great wife and a great life, but because I know the love of Jesus. All those other things are wonderful, but I would still be empty inside without Jesus. I didn't know love till I knew Jesus personally.

For More Information contact:
        Rob McGrath
        House of the Good Shepherd,
        7670 Sixth Street,
        Burnaby, B.C.
        V3N 3M7

Armed Robbery Gone Wrong

The Life

of

GERRY BEZANSON

The morning of December 13, 1971, the RCMP (Royal Canadian Mounted Police) knocked on our door. One of the officers said, "Are you Otto Bezanson?" and my dad replied, "yes". I remember standing under my dad's arm. He continued, "Mr. Bezanson, I have some bad news for you. Last night a tragedy took place. Your wife has been killed." The man she was traveling with has turned himself in to the police and confessed that he caused your wife's death. She is dead and will not be coming home. I'm sorry to have to deliver this bad news to you." I couldn't believe my mother was never coming home again. I was only eleven years old. I ran out the back door and through the woods sobbing as the reality began to sink in.

How could this happen? Let me tell you my story. My mother's name was Dorothy Lutz. She was from Aylesford in the Annapolis Valley, Nova Scotia in Eastern Canada. My

Mother – Dorothy Bezanson,
Gerry 3, Brian 7, 1963

dad, Otto Bezanson was from New Ross, on the south shore of Nova Scotia. He moved to the Annapolis Valley after marrying my mother. He purchased a property in a small community called Auburn.

My mother had six children, Otto Jr., Sandra, Willis, Sheila, Brian and I was the youngest. Today we all live in the Annapolis Valley and are back together as a family. We lived in the last house on a dirt road that backed into the pine trees. Most of my brothers and sisters had grown up and moved away by the time I was 10 years old.

My dad, after recovering from TB, had a large salvage business. I would often play in the old cars pretending to be a race car driver. For some reason I always imagined I was outrunning the police. I was always the bad guy, always putting myself into a negative attitude. As I grew up I would help in the business with my brothers but I always felt that I never really fit in. I had become a loner.

My Dad also worked at the Army Base as a cook for many years. He also used to bootleg liquor. We had all sorts of characters coming to our home day and night to buy liquor. My parents were heavy drinkers and had lots of parties. With the alcohol came the swearing, and fighting. I thought that this was the norm because of other homes I visited with my dad and the same things were going on. I heard and saw things that a little boy should never see or hear.

My mom and dad would fight and my mother would suffer. One time he broke her arm by throwing her across the room. Fishing was my escape from reality. I would fish for hours, especially on weekends when I knew they would be partying. When I came home, proud of my catch, my dad didn't even acknowledge it. I remember if I tried to give him a hug to say good night, he would put up his arm if I came close. That was unacceptable in our home.

My mom made every effort to care for me. One evening she was tucking me into bed and I could smell alcohol on her breath, but she said to me, "Gerry I want you to know that God loves you." I thought this was odd coming from an alcoholic, who had never lived that life, but had a knowledge of God and His love. She would sometimes pray with me at night and our only prayer was, "Now I lay me down to sleep, I pray the Lord my soul to keep. If I should die before I wake, I pray the Lord my soul to take".

The minimal amount of knowledge I had about God came from the prayers that we had together and when she shared her heart with me. Even when my mom had been beaten and bloodied, she would still say, "Gerry, be a good boy. Grow up to be a good man and don't treat women badly. You must love and respect them. Promise you'll grow up to be something in life". I always wanted to accomplish great things in life and I promised my mother I would finish school.

But I didn't fit in at school either. I went to St. Mary's Elementary School and while waiting for the bus, the older kids would call me names and put me down because of where we lived. It was a home where we took baths in wash tubs and had an outhouse. We also had pigs and chicken in the barn and raised some of our own food. We lived on one side of the tracks and most of the village was on the other.

As a child I always had a fear that my parents would drink and then drive and one day they wouldn't come home. They would be killed in a car accident or fight. There were many nights where I was sick to my stomach with worry. At such a young age, I developed bleeding ulcers which was partly due to worry and my beginning to drink at the age of 12.

One evening, December 12, 1971, there was a party in our home. My dad was selling liquor and he ran out. There was a poker game going on, and I was sitting on my dad's knee. I had just got him the last beer. There was a pot of money on the table from the poker game. A friend of the family was there and he had just been released from the local men's correctional facility. He was in there for domestic violence and was on parole. Unbeknownst to us, he had hot-wired his brother-in-law's car and drove it to our home while he was drinking.

When we ran out of liquor, my dad asked this man to go to another bootlegger who was five minutes away to get a case of beer. He agreed and my dad sent my mother with him. My brother had taken our car to go to work so that's why dad sent this other fellow. We didn't know that the car he was driving wasn't his. My mother went with him and I remember her bending down and kissing me on the cheek. This was odd because she didn't do that if she was stepping out for the evening, but that night she did. A blizzard came up and they never returned. We feared that there had been a car accident.

About 2:00 o'clock in the morning, my father and I walked to this fellow's home through the deep snow. When we arrived, we were told that they had been there but he had no liquor so he sent them to another bootlegger. So we went to the next bootlegger and we were told that they had been there as well, but he also had no liquor and sent them on. We went home not sure of what had become of them.

After hearing the news from the RCMP and crying it out in the woods, I returned home and found my brothers and sisters and other family members there. For the next three days I was in a no-man's land.

We buried my mom on December 15, 1971. I recall that cold, cloudy, winter day, and that was how I felt inside. I remember as her casket was lowered into the ground, I made a fist and pointed it to the sky and said out loud, "There is no God". And, at that point, something changed inside of me. I remember feeling hate which gave me a sense of power, even though I was powerless. I began to walk in hatred, anger, blame and in bitterness.

I remember how it felt to come back to school after my mother's funeral. Everyone stared at me. They all knew what had happened because it was in the newspapers as the man had to go on trial. This guy, who was on parole, had stolen his brother-in-law's car, been pro-violation drinking, and now admitted that he had gotten into a conflict with my mother, and had beaten her to death. We were in a very small town so the court situation was very well known. It was on the front pages of the newspapers during the months leading up to the trial. We were "that Bezanson family".

The trial ensued and the man actually walked after three months. He got off for the murder of my mother and I was extremely angry. I was so confused. How could the justice system allow such an obvious injustice? How can people stand by and allow such a thing to happen? We felt powerless. We were very poor and the salvage business did not provide a lot of money and much of the money went into drinking. We didn't have enough to hire a good lawyer to pursue the case. The man walked even after he gave a signed confession.

I began to cause problems at school. Some teachers tried to help me. I found out later that they were Christian ladies who loved me and prayed for me but there was so much anger and bitterness in me that no-one could reach me. Many believed I was incorrigible and beyond help. They believed things would get worse for me because of my choices. It was a dark time in my childhood, and it got darker as time progressed.

Sometimes when teachers tried to help, there was this thing inside of me which caused me to laugh hysterically in their faces. This thing would come up out of my belly and begin to mock and make fun of them. It had no respect for anyone in authority, especially the police, the law, the teachers, and my dad (I had begun to rebel against him to the extreme). There was an out-of-control laughter that rose up out of me. It was a diabolical, cynical, sarcastic, mocking spirit to these people in authority over me. Perhaps it was that, that made me say, "you can't control me, I am in control of my own life now". I pushed anyone with caring and compassion away because I didn't care about me anymore. Suicide was on my mind.

My dad still bootlegged so there was always liquor around. My dad tried to make up for the lost years. He bought me scale models of cars, planes and boats. I liked putting them together and it was a good pastime. He was desperately trying to recapture the lost years. I couldn't believe my dad had bought me a brand new, green, CCM bicycle, for no occasion. I had never had anything new in my whole life except maybe at Christmas. It was a beautiful bike and I loved it.

He started to go fishing with me, but I wasn't interested any more. I had already started stealing, hanging around with the wrong crowd, drinking every weekend, smoking marijuana, hash and taking acid. We were coming into the early 70's and acid was a big thing at that time. I was in high school and other kids were doing it. I was making new friends and connections. I met drug dealers, and those involved in break and enters. My negative peer group was expanding. I was game for anything. It didn't really matter what happened to my life. The more excitement I could find, the better.

I quit school at 16 and was working at some odd jobs, on farms and different seasonal jobs. They'd only last for a pay cheque or two and then I'd go out and party for a weekend. I'd lose the job or I'd quit. I'd take my pay on Friday night and go party all weekend and realize when I woke up on Monday what a big mistake I had made.

I found out quickly that I was developing an expensive lifestyle. Stealing and break and enters began to happen. Most of the time I was alone. On a few occasions I had partners. The break and enters continued and I found I could get money and items I could resell. I lived in the fast lane and I was on easy street. I felt the world owed me something.

I began to break and enter in homes and businesses and eventually progressed to armed robbery. One night, a friend and I met up at the pool hall. We had a few joints and some beers. I asked him if he'd like to make some easy cash. He said, "sure". He wasn't a criminal type but, being his friend, he kinda looked up to me. He asked me what were we going to do. I told him he would find out when we got there.

We got into my 1966 Chevy. I'd already packed nylon stockings to hide our identities should we be seen during the commission of the offense. I had a large baseball bat size stick or club that I had made, and I would use it as an intimidating factor should I have a confrontation with anyone. I never had to use a weapon. It was only for threatening purposes. In break and enters, usually nobody was there. I would case the place to get the person's routine down so I wouldn't have any confrontations.

This one night my friend and I parked under a bridge in the country. I already knew which house I was going to rob. My friend asked, "What are we doing here? I thought we were going to make some bucks." I told him to shut up and told him to put a stocking mask on. I had gloves and wool socks to cover my army boots so I wouldn't leave footprints. We went across a field to a home which was in darkness.

We went in and found out that there was a man at home and we surprised him. We were surprised as well, as we didn't expect him to be there. A struggle ensued and I struck the man over the eye with the club and he fell back on his bed. I found $800 and we left the scene.

As we left, the man was rolling around on his bed and moaning. I could see blood trickling down his face so I knew I had hurt him quite badly. We left in a hurry, got in my vehicle, took off the nylon stockings and went to a nearby gravel pit. We split the money down the middle and went on to party the rest of the night.

When I woke up the next morning, after I had been drinking and smoking a lot of dope, I went out to my Chevy to clean it. I opened the trunk and saw the blood covered club. Then I started remembering what had happened the night before. I was quite foggy at first. Then I realized that I really hurt the man. I was hoping and praying that he'd be all right. I cleaned out the vehicle and disposed of the club and stockings on a back woods road. I threw the empty billfold into a brook.

The next day I drove to the service station in Auburn, parked the car, and was drinking a beer in the parking lot. I noticed some police vehicles, a fingerprint wagon, a few dogs and policemen across the street. They were combing the area behind the grocery store, which led to the road where the man's home was located. They proceeded towards his property. I wondered what all the police activity was about. This was a small town and you didn't often see that kind of stuff. Then it clicked, it was the direction to the home I had robbed. I asked the service station attendant what was going on with all the police in town. He said, "Oh you haven't heard, the gentleman who lived on that road was found dead by his neighbour this morning. They suspect foul play."

It hit me then right in my guts. "Oh my God, did I kill this man?" This was my first thought, my first reaction. I must have done it. I sat in my car and watched the police just a few hundred feet away combing the area as they began to investigate this crime.

The police moved on to continue their investigation. My partner in the crime suggested we pack up and head out west. I said, "No, that's exactly what the police would be looking for. Let's just lay low and take it easy".

Later on, they ruled out foul play and said "cause of death - natural causes". It threw me for a loop. Natural causes how could that be? I didn't dare ask or be too curious or I would give myself away. It left a real question mark in my mind. It played on my mind that I must have caused this man's death. They suspected foul play. There must have been some reason to support that or they wouldn't say it. Even the newspapers said he died in some suspicious way.

This tortured and ate away at me for months. I was only 17 years old, but I had been drinking for about two solid years. I wasn't drunk all the time but I was certainly an alcoholic.

In 1976, I met a girl named Kim Bruce. Her parents owned the local grocery store. We spent time at her parents' home and store. We watched hockey with her dad. I knew when I met and fell in love with her that she was different. There was something special about her. We'd been going together for about a year when she became a Christian. She went to Peter Youngren's Revival Crusade in Sackville, Nova Scotia. He was preaching at a big tent meeting and doing revival services. She had given her heart to the Lord.

She told me that she and her parents had given their

hearts to Jesus and become Christians. I said, "You haven't gone and got religious on me have you?". I shoved her away and said I didn't want to hear that stuff. After I pushed her away, she began to cry and said, "Gerry, you need the Lord. I know you're going down the wrong path. I don't know exactly what you are involved in, but you need Jesus in your life". I thought I would intimidate her and said, "Listen, you've got to make a choice. If you love me, walk away from this Jesus. You've got to turn your back on this religion because you're going over the deep end." I really thought she would pick me because we had been going together for a full year. She looked at me and cried and said, "Please don't ask me to make this choice".

She was fourteen when I met her. Now she was fifteen and I was seventeen and she was being forced to make a choice - to deny Jesus for me, her boyfriend. She said, "I don't want to make this choice, but if you force me to, I'll choose Jesus because He's real and He's awesome and you need Him in your life". I pushed her away and said, "I don't want anything to do with you or with your God. There is no God". I walked away with an emptiness inside, knowing I had done the wrong thing but I couldn't allow my pride to be broken. I went away miserable.

For three months she wrote me long letters over ten pages long. She kept telling me, "Jesus loves you. I'm praying for you. Jesus loves you. I love you. You need Jesus, He's the answer". Her mom and dad began to pray for me. There were twenty-one family members and friends that were saved that year. Revival swept through the community and many of those family members began to attend the local Pentecostal Church.

One Saturday morning, I woke up very depressed. I was going through bouts of depression at the time. I was still living at home. One day I got up and looked up over my bed where I had a gun rack. I had a .22 bolt action rifle with a scope. I became fixed on the rifle. I took the rifle down. It was as if I were in the twilight zone. I took one bullet out of the box, pulled the bolt back, put the bullet in the chamber, took a joint, a cold bottle of beer and the rifle and walked out the back door. It was October 1977, I walked back through the field and saw the colours of trees were beautiful. I went into the meadow where I spent a lot of time alone as a child.

I sat and drank my beer, smoked my joint and looked at the gun and thought, "If I ever get caught for this crime, even though it was an accident and I never meant for it to happen, I would just pull the trigger". I wanted to put myself out of my torment. I put the barrel of the gun in my mouth, fumbled for the trigger. I put my thumb on the trigger and said, "This is it!". As I sat there that morning, I wasn't hallucinating. I only had one joint and one beer and I was in my right mind when I heard a voice. At first I thought my dad had followed me. The voice simply said, "Wait". I looked around and nobody was there. I shook it off and didn't think much of it. I was going to pull the trigger and I heard, "Wait" for a second time. I heard it again. By the third "Wait" I thought there is something going on. I got up and took off for home. I knew I wasn't crazy, something was going on.

A couple of days after this suicide attempt, I received a phone call from my ex-girlfriend. She wanted me to go to church with her. I said, "No way". She wanted me to go with her to another Peter Youngren tent meeting as he was preaching in Sackville again. So I went to this tent meeting. All I can remember was laughter, arms raised, and some people crying. They seemed to be so happy. They seemed so alive. I'd never been around people like that before.

A man began to speak in tongues (1 Cor. 14) and I felt a strange sense of awe, of reverence. I didn't know for what or for whom, but there was something that witnessed in my spirit. I thought Peter Youngren was pretty cool, because as a Swede, he had an accent, and when he said, "Amen" it sounded more like "Hey Man". That was a cool phrase we used as teenagers in the seventies. I didn't know anything about church or its' lingo so I thought Hey Man was pretty cool.

As we came home, I started thinking for the first time. "What if I've been wrong? What if my dad's been wrong? What if there really is a God?" I started asking myself, "How did the moon get there? How did the stars get there? How did we get here?" Creation began to speak to me and challenge my thoughts, my beliefs, and my value system.

A few weeks later, I got a call from my ex-girlfriend on Sunday morning and she wanted me to go to church with her and I said, "No way". Then her dad called and said, "Come on Gerry, go with us just one more time. I really believe you'll get something out of church this morning". He persisted even after I said no. I had a lot of respect for Clinton Bruce as he had taken me under his wing and treated me well. I finally said, "Okay, I'll go for you. Just this one time". I made a vow that this would be the last time.

We went to the little Pentecostal Church in the country. I wore my leather jacket, biker boots and dark glasses. I was full of attitude and arrogance. The Worship Service began and people had uplifted hands, some were crying and some were dancing in the aisle, some were laughing and I thought, "Man these people are wacked out. I've got to get home and get a beer into me".

Yet, at the same time in the church, I felt something. I felt loved. I felt cared for. People paid attention to me and hugged me and said, "God bless you" and "glad to have you here today". I wondered why. They're a bunch of phonies because that's what I believed about everybody in church.

Then as the preacher, Earl Murdock was preaching, he stopped, closed his Bible and said, "You know who you are and I have a word for you this morning and the word is this: you are here and you are on the run (and I had been)". That caused the hairs on my neck to stand up. Who was he talking to? There were a bunch of gray-haired ladies, some young kids and a few teenagers who looked like pretty good kids. Then he said, "You are on the run from God but you can't run from God and you can't hide from God".

I could feel a conviction in my spirit. I had been running from God and hiding from the law and I felt like I couldn't keep going this way. Then came the final straw. He said, "You've come to the end of yourself, you don't want to do this any more. You don't want to run from God anymore. You have even considered taking your own life to end it all. I want to tell you today, that Jesus is the answer for your life".

The next thing I knew I was at the front of the church on my face before God weeping like a baby. Rivers began to flow through me, washing and purging me from the violence, the rage, the hatred and the sin. I began to feel like something was happening on the inside. I began to feel clean and I began to feel whole. Scripture says, "Old things are passed away, and behold all things become new". We are new creatures in Christ Jesus, a new creation.

God does know best and He knows what we must go through to get us to where He wants us. People gathered around me and one of the Deacons, Sidney Spurrell spent time with me. He prayed with me and later became a good friend. Pastor Earl Murdock also prayed with me and we became very close. I began to confide in him, but I never told him or my girlfriend about the robbery and the man that had been killed. Only my partner and I knew about that.

Even after I gave my life to the Lord that morning, I went back to the world to test things out for three or four months. I hung out at the pool hall, drank a few beers and smoked a few joints. I never found the satisfaction I'd had before. Once I came to know Jesus there was no going back I knew there was only one direction. Back to the arms of the Lord Jesus.

Finally, I returned to church one Sunday night. I had been drinking and was stumbling. At the end of the service the Pastor came down to the back of the church, took my hand and we walked to the front. I knew that tonight was the night. It was December, 1977 and with a commitment in my heart, I said, "Lord Jesus I know I need you. I am a sinner. Come into my heart. Transform me. Change me. Make me the man you want me to be".

The devil on my shoulder said, "What about your friends, what will they say?". At that point I said out loud, "Lord God I know the devil is saying that I can't do this, that I am weak, but with your help I can. I don't care what my friends say". I knew that night that I would never take a drink of alcohol or a toke again. I was tempted for about a year but I kept submitting to the Lord. God broke through and worked a miracle in my life. He delivered me from the chains of alcohol, drug addiction and crime.

I got off the streets, got my own place and started work at a local hospital as a cleaner. For the first time in my life, I got a pay cheque and it felt great that I had earned money and I didn't have the urge to take it and go on a binge.

My girlfriend and I got back together. We began going to church together; Bible study on Wednesday night; youth group on Friday night; Sunday morning and Sunday night church; and youth rallies all around the Maritimes. We went to everything. We wanted all the Lord had for us. I began to grow strong in God. A year or so after becoming a Christian, about 1979, I became the Youth Leader at Trinity Pentecostal Church. It was a new church we built across the street from the old converted pizza parlour church. I helped build this new church with my own hands as did many others, including the pastor.

Now I went into taverns and jails with my Bible, sharing the Gospel with my friends. I began to share by going door-to-door. I didn't know a lot about the Bible but I knew that Jesus was able to transform hearts and lives. People that knew me in the community couldn't believe the change in my life.

One night back at my Dad's place, there was a party going on. I had been back to visit and some old friends were there. They were drinking and tried to force me to drink a beer but I kept spitting it out. They kept saying, "Do you think you are better than us?". I said, "No, I just don't want this lifestyle any more. I'm not condemning you." Their consciences were bothering them. They were blowing marijuana smoke in my face but there was no way I would take the joint.

I continued as a youth leader and the group grew from just a couple to twenty-two or twenty-three teenagers to young adults. We would spend times around the altar at night praying for one another and we would bring other young people in and pray for them. I had a deep desire to teach and preach and I felt I was called to the ministry. I applied to the Bible College in Peterborough, Ontario. I didn't know how I'd pay for it or how it would work, I just knew I wanted to initiate something in preparing for the ministry

In the meantime, Kim and I were still dating. I had my little apartment and I proposed to her. We were engaged to get married and a lot of things were happening fast, but I wanted to go this route. I felt that this was what God was doing in my life. It was good and it was blessing after blessing. My life began to be transformed before my eyes. My dad didn't know quite what to think of this. He wasn't really fond of the idea of my becoming a Christian, but he never really opposed it too strongly.

I waited for a response from the Bible College. One day when I was going to the mail box, I said to Kim, "I know my acceptance letter will be there but I know that their answer will be no". She said, "How do you know?". I said, "The Lord just told me, that's not the way He wants me to go" but He is still calling me to the ministry.

I went to the mail box and there was a letter from the Bible College saying, "You have been rejected because, you were too late. You can reapply next year." I was devastated. A year seemed a long time. I knew it would be difficult as I had dropped out of school halfway through Grade 10. But I thought, "Okay Lord, maybe you have some other plans".

Kim and I were married in 1981 and a year later, God blessed us with a baby boy, Justin Corey Bezanson.

One day, a detective from the Halifax Homicide Department and a Police Sergeant came to where I worked wanting to ask me some questions about 1977. I knew right away that was the date of the event that had tormented me. I had always wanted to deal with it but never had the courage to come forward. In my heart, I knew, as a Christian, that this would happen someday. I would have to come clean, tell the truth so I could move on. I began to confess to them that I had committed this crime.

I was arrested December 3, 1982 and went to the King's Correctional Centre. My wife came to visit me. She brought my son to visit me one day and it was so difficult sitting behind a screen having no contact with my family. About five months later in May of 1983, the case went to trial. I had confessed to the armed robbery and assault with a weapon but I knew the gentleman was alive when we left. I wanted to know what really happened. It had been almost six years since the crime. There were details that I wasn't aware of, and I wanted to clarify my level of responsibility.

It was a five day trial. Many facts came out that brought questions to my mind and my lawyer's minds. There was a possibility that another party was involved, after my partner and I left the house.

Evidence was being presented, that thousands of dollars in different wallets and bags were missing when the police arrived and searched the house. The body was found in a different place. Incredible facts surfaced.

However, I was found guilty of armed robbery and second degree murder. My partner received eight years for manslaughter for becoming a Crown witness to testify against me. I was given ten years to life to be served in Dorchester Penitentiary in New Brunswick. I was taken to a place of maximum security in King's Correctional Centre and from there I was transferred to Dorchester a few days after my sentencing. I was transported in cuffs and shackles and given the number ...FPS #4674.

We traveled the four hour trip to New Brunswick on December 23, 1983. We were released from the van and as we shuffled up to the huge set of stairs into the prison, the sheriff said, "Stop here for a moment fellas". He said, "Look to your right". To our right was a long concrete wall which was 40 feet high leading to a tower at the corner of the prison. Then he said, "Look to your left". There was another long wall with a tower in the corner as well.

We looked at him and he said, Take a good, long, look because this is where you're going to be for a long time. It will be a very long time before you ever see daylight on the outside of this prison". He laughed and sneered. I thought to myself, "We're in for trouble. There's absolutely no compassion in this man. Perhaps he's done this so many times before that he's become desensitized and insensitive to others' needs and circumstances".

The young lad with me was only eighteen years old and I was twenty-three. Here we were, both first-timers going into a prison. We went into the prison with the Sheriff and two guards who escorted us to the basement area which was called A & D (Admission and Discharge). We were stripped naked. Our personal effects were put into an envelope, boxed and sent home. We were given prison pants and shirt and numbers. We were placed in a holding cell until we could be escorted to D Range. I was put into a cell in D5, a reception range and the lad who was with me in the van was a few cells down.

That night was one of the longest nights of my life. I began to question the Lord, saying, "God are you still with me? Will You carry me through? My wife is gone. I've left her behind. My baby son, my job, my freedom, the love and support of a Christian Church family, my father, brothers and sisters, it's all gone ... where is my life going?".

I was reminded of the story of Joseph in the Bible, who

141

was sold into slavery by his brothers. I thought about that story because Joseph went through so much, yet in the end God allowed the circumstances to elevate him from a low place to a high level of responsibility, to lead and preserve a nation from famine. I thought perhaps there was a purpose in my life for being here.

I was sentenced to life in prison with only the hope of parole maybe in ten years. The Scripture that I really built on and held to was Romans 8:28 "and we do know that all things work together for good to those who love God and are called according to His purpose". I held onto that in those early days, weeks, months and years believing that God would somehow bring good out of this situation.

I'll never forget the next morning, a Salvation Army officer came down, tapped on the bars and I woke up and looked at him. He introduced himself as the Chaplain from the Salvation Army here at Dorchester. I'd like you to come to the chapel with me and I'd like to talk with you since you're a new inmate here". He called to the guard and said, "Key up", and the guard spun the wheel which moved the rails to open the doors in the cells and my door was opening. He escorted me to the chapel, a place called The Upper Room.

The Chaplain was a terrific man of God. He was not just a knowledgeable man in the Word of God, but also how the mind, heart and soul works in an inmate, especially the long-termers and lifers. This man and I connected right away. I felt I had a friend in this Chaplain. He allowed me a phone call to my wife from the phone in the Chapel. Later I returned to my cell. It was the 24th of December, Christmas Eve.

I'd read my Bible each day and prayed. One night I was sitting on my bunk and I heard banging and screaming. The next thing I knew, it started up on my whole range. Soon they were screaming and pounding on pipes all through the different ranges. Then the fluorescent bulbs were being smashed and I began to see smoke. People were ripping mattresses up and stuffing them between the bars and beginning to burn them. Water began to flow down our range, into my cell. Toilets had been broken off. Pipes were busted and water was pouring everywhere. I couldn't understand what was happening. This was the beginning of orientation for me into a Federal Penitentiary system. This was a prison riot!

Guards came up with their shields, billy clubs and mace. They dragged inmates out of their cells and took them to the Hole, a place in the lower section of the prison for punishment. The water in my cell was about two inches deep. I stayed up on my bunk. The smoke came in and I kept my face covered with my pillow. I was panicking and praying, "My God, what have I gotten myself into?" I never dreamt prison would be like this.

I started to become very aware of my surroundings, and the people that were on my range (about 28 cells). I began to watch my back and all around me. I began to size up people and figure them out. I watched body language and facial expressions, and what was in their eyes.

The first month was the most difficult because a lot of things happened. Suicides happen more around Christmas time. A man hung himself in his cell with a bed sheet. It brought the morale of the institution down. It affected everyone.

I entered prison in the winter time. In New Brunswick there's lots of snow storms and cold weather. The winds would blow inside the prison wall and howl. I wore only a pair of green institutional coveralls and underwear, that was all. I had no t-shirt and the coveralls were way too big for me. The sneakers I had were size 11. There were no laces so they fell off my feet. Wearing only these garments, we had to go outdoors for recreation for at least fifteen minutes to half an hour a day.

We'd go down five flights of stairs to the back yard which was a fenced area for recreation. Guys would go out and have a smoke and huddle with each other. We would walk around the track, beating a path in the snow, and following each other. We were like caged animals. There was a leader and everyone would follow him. We went around in a circle, going nowhere. You had to stay out for the duration of rec time.

I was only on D Side for a couple of weeks and then they moved me to Reception & Orientation. I had now been inside for two and half months. A correctional officer came to my door and said, "Bezanson, you have an appointment with your case worker". I thought, "My case worker, who's that?".

The officer took me downstairs. I went to the visiting room and there were officers and the case worker.

I sat in front of this man and we introduced ourselves. He opened my file, saw that I was doing ten years to life and said, "Mr. Bezanson, I need to be straight with you. You are doing a life term. You'll probably do at least twelve to fifteen years before you get out. Most lifers do twelve or more because they usually act up for three or four years and then they start to realize that they are doing themselves more harm. You have come into the system and you are a born-again Christian. You have some standards and values in your life that you never had before. You are alcohol and drug free. You are crime free from what we can tell from the Police Reports, the Community Assessment Report and the Parole Officers Report and we just don't see a whole lot that we can do with you. Unfortunately you are here to do at least ten years. You will have to go out into the population and find your own way. Get into a school program or learn a trade. There is just no point in your coming back to see me at least not for another five years. "

I said, "What do you mean, five years, you're my case worker right? You're supposed to be helping me". He said, "I will help you as much as I can but there are other men doing shorter sentences and I have to work with them first". I really felt insignificant. What was happening to me? I couldn't get any passes out of the institution. He just told me to come back in five years when we could talk about a transfer to a medium security prison. I left that place feeling lower than the floor that I walked on. My heart sunk beneath my feet. I went back in my cell and I cried out, "God where are you now? I can't believe this is happening to me."

I finally determined within myself and thought whatever comes, comes. I'm not a big fella, about 128 lbs., very slim, not many muscles, but whatever comes, comes, Whatever I have to face Lord, I will face. Whether I live or die, Lord I give my life to you afresh. I rededicated my life right there in that prison cell on my knees. I said, "I want to live for truth. Help me God to live for You while I am in this prison and whatever prisons I end up in. If something happens that I get caught in a riot, or have a problem or fight with another individual, it happens. (They don't deal with fists, they deal with weapons, clubs, chains, weight bars, knives, and shivs) Lord I will not carry a weapon to defend myself, no matter what the cost, I will not pick up a weapon again".

I went to one of the guards and said, "I know I'll eventually be released into population but I don't want to wait any longer. I want to sign myself out into population now. Usually you spend a couple of months in orientation but I couldn't stand it, so I signed a waiver to get into population sooner. I want to begin my life and my sentence here". I wanted to get into a school program or a work program that would better me and help me to settle in and find my place in the Penitentiary. I wanted to find a routine that would help my time go by a lot better. They put me on C5 Range which is a non-productive range. I was only there for a couple of weeks and then they transferred me down to C2 Range, Cell 18.

I was just getting settled in with my bed roll and my Bible, when the Chaplain came along. He prayed with me and I said, "I really appreciate you. You are about the only light in this darkness. You are the only hope there is in this hole". I thanked him for being in the prison, as a Minister of the Gospel of Jesus Christ.

On C2, I could go to the Chapel programs. I went to the Tuesday night fellowships when volunteers would come in from Moncton, N. B. and Amherst, N.S. This was a real source of encouragement, a real building up of the inner man by these Christian people. Sometimes they even brought their children. I thought, "Wow, there must be a real sense of trust here".

In the first six months in Dorchester, I got my Grade 12 GED. I also worked as a cleaner in the Chapel which gave me a little more contact with the programs and events that took place in there. One day I had a group of four guys come to the Community Centre's barred door which led into the Chapel. They called me over and said, "Hey you, Bezanson". My case was in the news before I went into prison. They told how I had been a Christian for many years, and then had been convicted for murder. It was an unusual situation. This muscular guy said, "Us guys came over to check you out. How can you be a Christian and be a murderer. God don't love murderers. He don't forgive murderers. How can you be a

Christian murderer?". I said, "It's like this. The Word of God says nobody is above anybody else and I am not a Christian murderer, I am a Christian who committed crimes. God has forgiven me and as far as God is concerned my slate is clean". The guy says, "I don't accept that. You're some kinda phony. Who do you think you are? You're just a convict like us".

I could sense the hostility and I said, "I don't know you and there are four of you and there is only one of me. It's like this, I'm going to be around for a long time and I imagine you guys will be too. I'll tell you what, if you think I'm phony, time will tell if I am real or not. You watch and see and let time be the factor". They cursed and walked away.

Other chaplains, besides the Salvation Army officer, that were there, were Pierre Allard, a Baptist minister and the Catholic Chaplain, Sister Gloria Boudreau who were a great source of support for me. These three individuals were constantly busy counseling with us men. The chapel was always packed out. I'd go to the chapel and I met lots of people.

At the chapel I met this biker. His name was John and he had been in prison for quite some time. He had a 25 to life sentence for murder when he was with the bikers. Now he was a born-again Christian who gave his life to the Lord in prison. There was a crew of us that used to walk around the prison wall, day and night, rain or snow, it didn't matter what the weather. We had our Bibles out and huddled under the yard's yellow orange light. We'd read Scriptures to one another. We'd encourage one another. We'd sing songs and hymns. You know the Word of God says, "Singing songs and hymns to ourselves, making melody in our heart to the King of Kings". That's what we did and these men became my friends. The men would often say, "Here comes John and his disciples".

Every November we would have Prisoners' Sunday. The prisoners would take the song service, and the preaching (I preached there twice behind the pulpit and God opened up doors for prison ministry). When I was in the King's Correctional Centre, before I was transferred to Dorchester in 1983, I was in the Maximum Security Wing, B Block and there was a great big man in for armed robbery. He was about 6'2" and about 260 lbs. I was watching the Billy Graham Crusade one night and he changed the channel on me. Well,

I changed it back. There was a conflict there. I went to my room and came back out later. He said, "What's your problem?". I said, "Look, I don't usually watch TV much but I'm watching this program". He started lipping off at me and I'd been told that I should back off and leave this guy alone. He's doing a long time and he's got a lot to think about. He's heading up to Dorchester soon. Don't cause him any trouble. This guy was quite big and he probably could have taken me.

I found lifers in the Federal System have a great deal of respect and sometimes that's used to manipulate others. They do their time. They have a belly full of time under their belt. They want to get out. On the range that night when this big armed robber was telling me to shut the t.v. off because he didn't want to hear that religious stuff, I didn't want any trouble either.

When it was finished, I went to my room and began to read the Word of God. I closed my door and was praying. The door burst open and he stood in the doorway. The whole doorway was filled with this man's body, he was so big. He looked at me and said, "Tell me something, why did you stand up to me?". I looked at him and I didn't have an answer. He asked if he could come into my cell. I was a bit reluctant. I figured he was up to no good so I prayed under my breath. I said, "Lord, my life is in your hands. If I can be used of You Father to reach another inmate, use me". God was bringing purpose in my life even in this chaotic situation.

This fella came in to my cell and sat down on my bunk. Another young man came and stood in the doorway and then another as well. Finally, there were five of us. I sat on my covered toilet and began to share the Gospel. I began to tell them about Luke 23:42, 43, about the two criminals who hung beside Jesus. I told them that one rejected Jesus and one accepted Jesus. One went to Hell and one went to Heaven. One was forgiven and one was not. I said, "This is the way. Jesus said He is the Way, the Truth and the Life". They let me pray with them in my cell that night.

I was in Dorchester Prison for approximately a year when my father-in-law, Clinton Bruce died of cancer. I put in for a TA (Temporary Absence) for the funeral. I wasn't eligible yet but the authorities at Dorchester granted my release but only with the escort of two guards. When I went out to the keeper's hall, the Head of Security said that I had to go with shackles and cuffs on . Even though it was something I was reluctant to do, I gave in to it because I felt my wife needed my support. I went to the Annapolis Valley to our home church for his funeral. When he died it was a real loss. We were more than just in-laws, we were really good friends. The few years that he had lived as a Christian had a real impact on my life.

I had my visits with my wife and son in the visiting room. My dad, brothers, and sisters all visited me. My Pastor and friends from the church also visited. One time my church came and we had a service in the Chapel.

In the years while I was in prison, my wife, Kim worked part-time but not all the time. There were times when she didn't have money and she has told me how God provided. She would go outside and there'd be a box of groceries on the doorstep or a cheque or cash in the mailbox . Our second child, Kari Beth Bezanson was born. Kim would tithe 10 per cent of her income even though she was a single mother raising two children. She was faithful to God and recognized the importance of giving to God what is rightfully His. Thus God has blessed her and the family. It is important for single mothers to know that if you are faithful to God in tithes and offerings, He will bless you.

I got involved in a Tuesday afternoon Bible Study with Rev. Allard and some of the other inmates. There was a large group of guys in the Bible Study. On Wednesday nights, a dear old saint named Olive Phinney, who had been a missionary in China for over thirty years, came to the prison. I attended her Wednesday night Bible Studies with some of the other inmates. She had such an incredible richness of knowledge and experience, and a love of Christ. She told us of how God brought her through many difficult times in China during the Communist regime. She just shared her faith and her experience which brought so much home to us men, some of whom were serving life terms. She was so precious to us all.

Another highlight of my incarceration that inspired me and gave me better insight into the purposes of God for my life was when a young man named Alan came to me and asked, "Are you Gerry Bezanson?". He said, "A friend of mine directed me to you and I want to ask you something. I

148

know that you are a Christian so I have to ask you this question". So I said, "Go ahead", and he said, "What do I have to do to be saved?". The tears ran down his face and he said, "I want to be a Christian. I know you're a Christian and I want to know the Lord like you do".

Well here we were in the middle of the prison yard with fellas laying around getting a sun tan, walking or jogging around the track, and playing softball and I was thinking what are we going to do. I have to find a place to pray. Alan kept asking me if we were going to pray. I kept on thinking, "Lord what do we do?" I had my Bible because I always carried the New Testament in my hip pocket. I pulled out my Bible and began to read some Scripture to him and show him some of the passages that tell us we need to repent and turn from our sin and turn to Jesus. He kept saying, "When do we pray? ". I thought he was a bit impatient. Finally he said, "Can't we pray?" I thought "Lord, I've got to find a place to pray". So I said, "Let's go for a walk and see if we can find a place to pray".

Alan was looking at me mysteriously and couldn't figure out why we couldn't just pray right there in the middle of the yard. This young man had no shame about praying to the Lord Jesus Christ in front of 300 or so convicts. We finally walked around B7 and although there were still lots of people around, he said, "Why can't we just pray?" I looked at him and said alright. I didn't know what people would think. We would draw a lot of attention to ourselves but this young man was eager and I didn't want the moment to pass. We knelt on the grassy hill and we prayed. He reached out and took me by the hand and he said, "I'm a homosexual!" I thought, "Oh my God what are the people going to think". Here I was, this homosexual had grabbed me by the hand and we are kneeling and praying.

I asked the Lord to help me humble my heart and I prayed that this young man was sincere in his desire for conversion. We prayed a simple prayer asking the Lord Jesus Christ to come into his life and change his heart; give him a new way of thinking, a new mind set. The Scripture says, "old things pass away and behold all things become new". When we had finished we looked at each other. He had tears running down his face, and was smiling from ear to ear. He just looked at me and said, "Wow!". He said that he had no idea he could feel so much peace with his sins forgiven.

Alan became one of our disciples. He became part of our group, John and his followers. He grew in the Lord. He found that his homosexuality was a problem and he was able to surrender that part of his life to the Lord. In 1994, I was thrilled to hear he was doing well and still serving the Lord.

Alan had a tremendous voice and this young, black man would sing in the prison yards, the songs that we sang in Chapel. He was unashamed of Jesus. He was so bold yet he was so gentle in his spirit. God used him mightily to lead many men to the Lord Jesus Christ.

One afternoon after Chapel, Alan and I were walking around the yard. While we were walking two other inmates came over and asked if they could speak to me. I said, "Sure". They said, "In private". So I told Alan to go on ahead. There was a larger man and a smaller one. The big man said, "Gerry we know you here in the prison and you seem like an okay guy and it would be an awful shame if something were to happen to you.". I said, "What are you talking about?". He replied, "Well, I see you running around with this young, black boy. Is he your new friend?". I said, "I don't know what you're driving at." "It's like this", he says, "Tonight this young man and his brother are going down". This meant he was going to get stabbed or piped. I asked him why and his answer showed he was a racist. He said it would be a shame if I got caught in the crossfire. Fear is a controlling factor in the prison system. For a moment fear gripped me. I just said, "Thanks pal for letting me know". As I turned and walked away, he smiled.

The Holy Spirit spoke to me and said "You are a traitor and a phony. You're going to let your brother in the Lord die because of his colour and your fear". I turned around and called the guys over and said, "I want to tell you something. When I was on the street, nobody ever picked my friends for me and I'm not about to let anybody pick my friends for me now". He made a signal that he was going to stab me and said, "You're going to get it". Alan asked me later what was going on and I told him what was happening. I told them that they were planning to get him and his brother that night. I told them that I didn't feel like I could abandon them now and I didn't feel like we needed to hide out in our cells. Alan contacted his brother who was a Muslim and he wanted to fight these guys.

I walked around the prison yard that night with my friend and several other Christians. We sang and prayed. God kept His hand of protection on us. This individual who had made the threats, had been up for several counts of murder. God gave me the strength to stand in face of danger. God miraculously worked things out that these individuals never did come through on their threats.

There was no shortage of violence in the prison system. There was a young man, 19 or 20 years old, who was very quiet and never bothered anyone. He was in his cell on B7 when a couple of inmates came in. One held him down and the other stabbed him. He was stabbed numerous times all because of a rumour that he had ratted someone out. They weren't sure but they had heard the rumour. The young man lived. A few weeks later he stepped into the yard and took his t-shirt off. He wanted everyone to see the holes in his back and chest. He stood there as a sign to the people that they had made a big mistake. He stood tall making a very powerful statement to the population. He was telling them that he was here to stay.

Another gentleman who worked in the kitchen was sitting at a table one night playing poker with several other lifers. Another inmate came up behind him, a small man, and stabbed him in the back four or five times.

We spent a lot of time walking in the prison yard. One day, there was a bunch of guys screaming and yelling. A white man had a baseball bat and he was coming after a black man. The black fella faced him, took the baseball bat and started chasing the white guy across the yard. He gave one swing with the baseball bat and knocked him to the ground. Then he stood over him with his foot on his back.

In the summer of 1985, I applied for a transfer to Springhill even though I knew I had only three years in the system. I was accepted, but not until November of 1985. On December 3, 1985, my transfer materialized and myself and several others went to Springhill, a reduced security facility. I was security level six and was reduced to security level four.

I was placed in reception at Springhill with 40 - 50 other

inmates. I went through orientation for six to eight weeks. Springhill had three electrified fences around the outside, four gun towers, and vehicles patrolled the perimeter of the prison. It was as secure as Dorchester without the three foot thick and forty foot high walls. Here, there was a lot of grassy fields. The units were laid out like an octagon with a courtyard in the middle. There were breezeways or corridors to go to the Chapel, dining room and hospital.

When I arrived in Springhill I felt that I needed a hobby so I got into leather craft. I began to make wallets and weight belts for weight lifters and saddle bags for bikers. There were people on the outside who were interested in my craft and my skills and I found I could generate a little money. I put it into my canteen account. Now I could provide some monies to my wife and son when they came up for our conjugal visits in the trailer. We could spend a weekend together. We'd arrange this for special times like my son's birthday, our anniversary or Christmas. I could give Kim money to pay for the gas for the car or her motel bill if she stayed overnight in town.

Then I got a job working at the Scott Paper Tree Nursery. Scott Paper was a local paper mill business. They grew trees on the prison property, transplanted them and then sent them off to the States on tractor-trailers. We used to make minimum wage of $4.80 an hour. I had to wait about a year and I finally got the job outside the fence. It was called a Temporary Day Parole Status. It wasn't a day parole but it gave me daily clearance for work purposes only. This was really unusual because I had done only four or five years of my sentence. At this point in my life, I believe God was making it clear to me that I had found favour in the eyes of the Lord and man.

Since I had kept my driver's license renewed, I was able to get a job as the mailman and drove the prison truck. I would go to the prison garage in the morning and get the keys to one of the new Chev trucks. I'd make my rounds picking up each unit's mail and take it to the outside gate. In the afternoons, I would come back and pick up at the outside gate and bring it to the library in the different units.

I was at Springhill for about three years and by now I had seven years in on my sentence. I put in for a transfer to a minimum security prison called Westmoreland Farm Camp. There were no walls and towers there.

In December, 1988, approximately six and a half to seven years after I had been charged and convicted, I transferred to Westmoreland. During my three years in Westmoreland, I was a canteen operator for about eighteen months. I handled cash and sales. It was real money here, whereas in the other prisons we had plastic coins for our monetary system. Over the years I worked out in the weight pit. I had a work-out partner, named Charlie. One night Charlie came to me and said, "I did it. I gave my life to the Lord". I had witnessed to him for quite some time and then finally, he gave his life to the Lord. There were many men who surrendered their hearts to Jesus in Westmoreland. God used me as I earned the respect of the men, as I spent time with them.

A man transferred from Springhill, and came into the canteen where I worked and said, "Do you remember Howard?" I used to play guitar and darts with him at Springhill. He told me Howard was dying of cancer in the hospital. I phoned him and said, "I'm sorry to hear about your ill health, I'll be praying for you". He said in a weak, trembling voice, "Little buddy, it's okay now. You don't have to pray for me now. I've claimed Jesus as my own". At 2:00 o'clock the next day, Howard passed away.

I had been out on several group escorted passes. Finally, I was granted a day parole to a halfway house in Halifax, Nova Scotia for violent offenders. I was released there on the last five day pass prior to my parole being granted. We'd take the train from New Brunswick and then a taxi to the halfway house. I had been there a few times prior to being granted day parole. I got there on this last five-day pass, and was told I would have a bed there and the parole board would probably grant my release in a couple of months. I had to go back and apply to the parole board. I called my wife to share the good news that I would be coming out on day parole in the next couple of months. I would be able to find a job and be with her. Things were looking up after a long incarceration.

I decided I would sign out of the halfway house and go downtown to the Scotia Square Mall. I did a little shopping then I felt someone tapping me on my shoulder. I turned around and saw a man in a blue uniform. He asked if I was Gerry Bezanson, and told me he was with Corrections Canada and had to take me back to the halfway house. I asked why but he said it was a long story and I would just have to trust him. I said, "No way pal. I don't know you and I'm not goin' nowhere with you." Here I am in the city, a country boy, fresh out of prison and here is this guy telling me I had to trust him and go with him. I said I didn't think so. He wasn't a policeman. He wasn't an officer. He was a representative of the Correctional System. He started to press the issue and told me I had to go with him or else. I still refused.

He sat me down at a coffee shop and said, "I have some bad news for you. Your last five-day assessment pass that was granted by the Parole Board has been run by the Parole System. They've noticed somewhere in the process of things, that an error had been made by the administration office in Dorchester Penitentiary when you were first admitted there in 1983. They made a computer mistake and miscalculated the time that you had in on your sentence when you arrived there. Anybody who's charged with murder, if convicted, their time starts from the day they are arrested, which is unlike other crimes. They said, "You were in and out on bail in that year after being charged. They calculated your sentence as though you had a full year in, but it was broken up in time. They've recalculated your sentence for that year and they found out that you have to be placed under arrest. You are unlawfully at large and all your passes were premature by at least 344 days. You were unlawfully at large on all these occasions. You are being placed under arrest and being put back into custody".

The fellow had come to take me back to the halfway house. The director there confirmed what the representative had told me. A correctional officer would be sent to pick me up and take me back to prison. I had to serve an additional 344 days.

Talk about being disheartened. I was numb with disappointment. Through it all I trusted the Lord and found that He really was the God of the mountain and the God of the valley.

When I finally returned to the Parole Board, the Chairman looked at me asked me why didn't I run. He said, "You didn't become violent, but you were very controlled, submitted to custody even though it wasn't your fault. You served your additional time without incident. Why?" I told him I was devastated because I had told my wife I was being released in a couple of months. However the most important thing was being able to witness to the Parole Board, the power of Jesus Christ and how He was real and stabilized me.

So against the recommendations of my Parole Officer and my Case Worker, I asked for a Christmas ten day pass first and then my day parole at the end of the ten day Christmas pass. He said, "We don't normally grant ten-day Christmas passes any more. Please leave the room as we need to talk". Ten minutes passed. They called us back in. My wife, Kim was with me. The Chairman said, "Gerry, we've granted you your ten-day Christmas pass. We've granted you a day parole to Carlton Centre Halfway House, and we congratulate you and wish you all the best in the years to come". Kim and I hugged and kissed and we both cried. I was so grateful that these people would give me a chance to prove myself to them. I went home for ten days and enjoyed Christmas with my family. I was released in January, 1991 to the Carleton Centre Annex.

In the course of my incarceration, I felt it was necessary and important, as a Christian, to make reconciliation and restitution wherever possible. Some of the money I saved up in prison was used for this. When I went home on one three-day pass, I went to all the victims of my crimes and confessed. I asked that they would accept dollar reimbursement to the value that I stole. Of all those individuals that I visited, not one pressed charges or accepted any financial reimbursement. A community hall that did things for the community, accepted $400 on behalf of the community from the 1970's when I robbed the place.

I left a letter in the mailbox, of the Kingston RCMP before returning to the prison farm camp, confessing to the places I had robbed. I told them of the people I had visited to make restitution. They had investigated many of the crimes they suspected I had committed. Two weeks later they wrote back saying the file on me was closed . I knew when I confessed to these crimes that I could be facing more time in prison, but I knew in my heart that I had to come clean and be truthful in every way. I felt God was calling me into ministry and honesty was of the utmost importance.

I was at the Carlton House for eighteen months and took construction work classes for six months. It was a training course for concrete construction, building basements for homes and businesses. For the final six months I transferred to New Minas at Taps (Turn Around Point Services) Halfway House which was about fifteen minutes from my home.

On November 12, 1993, I was released home on full parole from TAPS Halfway House in Nova Scotia. I remember the first week I was home and it was wonderful. I was still working doing concrete basements. One night, we were at Trinity Pentecostal Church, our home church when a young man and woman came into the meeting wearing long trench coats. They had long, streaked purple, green and red hair, and earrings. They were carrying backpacks. I invited them to sit with my wife and I, but they didn't really feel comfortable so they sat at the end of a pew.

There were two other elderly women in that row. As they went to sit down the elderly women moved way over to be away from these young people. It really hurt me and I can only imagine how these young people must have felt. The women kinda curled their noses up at these young people and it bothered me. I said to Kim, "I've been talking about that for years, while I was in prison and before that". We need a place where these people would be loved and accepted." She looked at me and said, "Gerry, either do something about it, if it is God's will or be quiet". There is an old saying in prison, 'put up or shut up' and that is what she said to me.

Within the next couple of days, my wife and I began to look in the community of Kingston for a building for a small drop-in centre to accommodate young people, street people, ex-inmates and their families. Everything was too expensive. Nothing seemed to be a fit. Then one day about a week later, a tiny storefront room became available. It had been a hardware store and then a coffee shop. One of the doctors next door at the clinic owned the building in this strip mall. I asked for the key so I could go in and look it over and I felt in my heart the Lord was saying, "This is it! ".

They wanted $428.00 a month for rent. We didn't have it. We had no church or government support. We had never done anything like this. We just knew in our hearts that we were to reach out to the people on the streets. I began to realize that God had called me to something far greater than I had ever dreamed while I was in prison. God's plans are bigger than our dreams and he gave me Jeremiah 29:11, "I know the thoughts I think towards you says the Lord. Thoughts of good and not evil. Thoughts of peace to give you a future and an expected end". I have held on to those words for years while I was in prison that God had great plans for my life.

I began to sense faith leaping in my spirit. God was beginning to peel back the layers and show me His hidden purposes for my life. Romans 8:28 "We know that all things work together for good to those who love God and are called according to His purpose". That began to take on new meaning for me. It became a reality. Maybe my past was for a greater purpose in God, that I might be able to identify with the people on the streets and reach them. God could use that which the enemy meant for evil.

I returned the key and told them that the place was just right for us. The doctor told me to just keep the keys. I began to tell him it would be a youth drop-in centre for street folks. We would have Christian music, meetings and free recreation for the youth of the community. I shared in brief, my life story. He said it was a terrific idea and who better to do it than me. I thanked him for the compliment. On December 21, we opened the doors to The Haven Drop-In Centre. The word Haven comes from Psalms 107 and talks about people who are weary and without hope and direction in life, drifting like the ocean waves in a storm and then God brings them to their desired haven.

Folks came to check us out. We had a small pool table that we had been able to purchase with money that people from our home church had given us to get us started. We had a coffee percolator, chairs, a table, dart board, and a few board games from home. The first of January came and I went to pay the rent but I had no money. I was thinking that if we didn't get enough money for support from the churches and the community businesses, I would pay it out of my own pocket because I was still working pouring concrete. About a week after we began to work cleaning up the facility, I couldn't pay for it myself because I was laid off. I had to trust God. It was really quite frightening. He would show me how great He is.

When I walked into the doctor's office to pay the rent, I didn't have a penny. As I was walking towards the counter where the secretary was sitting, I heard the Spirit of God say to me, "It's my problem, it's not yours. You're just to oversee it. I'll take care of other responsibilities". I felt a peace come over me. The secretary said, "It's rent time isn't it? Well not to worry, the good doctor said the first months rent is free ". It's the doctor's way of saying, "Congratulations and welcome to the community".

Young people began to trickle in from surrounding communities as well as some curiosity seekers. Moms and dads dropped in, and soon we had families coming to the Haven. The District Office of the church denomination, with whom I am associated, asked me to fill in and do some pulpit supply because I was quite active in street evangelism before I went to prison. I agreed and I filled in at one church for three months. I met a couple there who became volunteers for four years at The Haven. Then we had more volunteers. This ministry was a "rolling up the sleeves" kind helping people in their need.

The Haven operated from 1993 to 1998 on Main Street. We met and helped hundreds of young people, families, drifters, drug addicts, alcoholics, people in abusive situations, ex-inmates, and young people in trouble with the law. With that, you are bound to run into difficulties. I am pleased to say that we never had to call the police over any situation with young people.

We expect people to come into the church to get what we have, but it is virtually impossible for hurting people to do that. Jesus gave us the commission to go to the highways and byways and seek out the lost. This is what we had attempted to do at The Haven. The rap time we had each Tuesday night became a intricate part of the Haven Drop-In Centre. Soon we were involved in group and individual counseling, family mediation, court appearances, and legal work.

In 1996, I received a phone call from Moncton, NB from the regional chaplain who wanted to know how things were going. John Tonks was the chaplain at Springhill Prison when I was there. He said, "I understand you're doing a good work in the Valley". I told him I go in and visit the Halfway House and take some of these men to church, and some to the Haven on Wednesday night. We had a hot supper on Wednesdays. We have Christian meetings with a speaker and counsel people. I told him that I had been cleared to go back to Springhill and Dorchester Prisons and have services there, and visit the fellas.

He said, "We've been wanting to get a chaplain down in that area for the last ten years. You are basically doing things that a community chaplain would do, would you like to consider the possibility of becoming our community chaplain for the Annapolis Valley area?". This was a shock to me.

I prayed and discussed it with my wife and a few days later I called him back and asked what would be required of me. He told me there were some courses and training that I would need to take, and just continuing the ministry we were already doing in community. They would give me a salary for being the community chaplain.

I was doing some odd jobs and my wife was working at a grocery store, but we were barely getting by. We had been faithful to God and now He was taking care of us financially. I accepted and began to travel to Moncton for the courses.

One day while attending the course, I received a phone call from my wife asking me to come home early because there were some problems at The Haven. Two men came in looking for me. The police are looking into it. They had a big duffel bag and there was some speculation that they had weapons. They threatened to kill you. I asked if she knew who they were. She said that the word was that they were ex-inmates.

I arrived home and called the RCMP. They had found out their names and told me who they were. I knew one of the men by name, but I had never had a problem with him. It made me quite nervous for both myself and my family. We took off that weekend to another area. We had the churches praying for us for wisdom and discernment. While we were away that weekend, I went to church by myself and said, "Lord, I need to know what to do. I've never run away from problems in my life. Here I have this mystery man who has an accusation against me. Please intervene and defend me and my family because Lord, we have trusted in You. As I was praying in my heart during the service, the Holy Spirit spoke to me and brought to my remembrance, Psalm 7 which is a prayer of David for deliverance from his enemies.

I was like King David, when he runs away after God had given him so many victories in his life. God was saying, "This person is nothing but a man, and he has made false accusations against you, I will make it right". After the service the Pastor's wife gave us a prophetic word that said, "the Lord said you will live and you shall not die. I am the Lord your God, I will keep you in the palm of my hand." We returned home.

The next night we opened The Haven and had a service. The police advised me not to open. I just told them it's time to flush them out because I can't live this way. That night we had quite a few of the Christian Bikers from Halifax. They arrived on their Harley-Davidsons wearing leather. They had long beards and pony tails. They parked their motorcycles out front and it was quite an impressive sight. They had their guitars out and were singing in The Haven and giving testimony to the Lord. People were coming in from the street and it was a good night. The Holy Spirit told me to step out into the street and meet this man face-to-face.

As I stepped out into the street. The Christian bikers followed me. We walked up the street together. The individual came out of the apartment building next door to The Haven. This is where he had been hiding out. He came out on the street. He was rolling up his sleeves. He said, "I suppose this is where I get the stuffing beat out of me". We were face-to-face and I recognized him. I called him by name and I said, "Listen, I'm not about to do any such thing to you, nor are these bikers. I'm here to face you to find out what's going on". He started laughing it off. All of a sudden, he stopped talking and was staring at me.

One of the bikers, took his hand and said, "In the name of Jesus, demon come out, demon of violence come out. demon of alcohol, drugs and violence come out.". He began to bind the spirits that were in this man's life, through the power of the name of Jesus. This man began to shake and tremble and he got choked up and had tears in his eyes. The bikers laid hands on him and began to pray for him.

He knew a number of these Christian bikers from years

of being in prison. He remembered how they would come in as volunteers. I prayed God's blessing on his life. I'll tell you it's a hard thing to do if you were to do it in your own strength but when the Holy Spirit is in control, He can do the supernatural. What the enemy meant for evil, God meant for good.

He shook my hand and asked me to forgive him. He told me he had been on heroin and boozing all week. He knew he shouldn't and was all messed up. He told me he had said some bad things about me. I told him I forgave him. God showed up on the streets. God shows up wherever He pleases if we but give Him an opportunity.

The Christian Bikers gave us an escort home. I wept all the way home because of the support and love of these Christian Bikers.

When God is at work, Satan fights back. We had several break-ins at The Haven. VCR's and equipment were stolen. Some people didn't want us in the community because I was an ex-inmate. The video store next door didn't want us there. People tried everything they could to get us out of town, because the conviction of God was on them. In all of this we were comfortable. The Apostle Paul says in Philippians 4: 11-13, "I've been through a lot, yet I know I can do all things through Christ who strengthens me".

After four and a half years of growth, in 1998, we came to the point where we just couldn't hold any more people. Some nights we had people standing on the sidewalk because we couldn't squeeze any more in. We needed a bigger facility. One evening we got a phone call from the Pastor of the church at the other end of town. He had heard that we had been asking the Lord for a bigger place. He told us he and his board members were praying, and as their group was getting smaller, he thought we might be interested in renting their larger facility. We got together and prayed about this.

Over a number of months we came to an agreement with the owners of the new facility, that we would rent with an option to buy. The facility was about 60 feet long and 25 feet wide and had two floors with a number of rooms, a sanctuary, kitchen, double bathrooms, a couple of offices, playroom, and a basement area for recreation. It was set in amongst a bunch of pine trees. It gave us lots of yard space and was near a new subdivision.

We moved in August, 1998 and expanded to a clothing depot, furniture depot, chaplain's office, a probation office rented by Corrections Canada, a recreation hall in the basement for the youth and a sanctuary where we began to have regular meetings each week. In the kitchen we provided hot meals every second and fourth Wednesday of the month. The ministry grew rapidly. We had our grand opening in October. We invited the Village Commissioner and some young people to take part in the grand opening and the local newspaper was there to take pictures. It was a moment to be recognized because God had done such a work in the face of such opposition. It was to His glory that this had been done.

Gerry – 1983 Dorchester Penitentiary

We didn't have the monies for the extra rent, heat and power but as we stepped out in faith, God increased the finances. Neil and Christine Barr of Lighthouse Ministries would come to be a very important part of what we do because our ministries had come together in prayer to follow the leading of the Lord. This has led to planting and establishing our own church in Nova Scotia.

God is using my life and my story in powerful ways I never thought possible. We think in our own mind, somebody else maybe, but certainly not me, but if we open our lives and make ourselves available for His purposes, there is nothing impossible to him who believes. We have seen the ministry expand and take deep roots. There is no limit to what God can do.

*Gerry and Kim
Bezanson
Justin and Kari*

Haven Ministries

In 1996, I was offered a position as the Protestant Chaplain at the Nova Scotia Young Offenders Prison. I had been hired as the chaplain, working part-time there about twenty hours per week. I go there to do programs, one-on-one counseling, group sessions, and lead the chapel service. I am the first lifer ever to become a chaplain in the Maritime Correctional System. With God all things are possible

I didn't get to attend Bible college but God prepared me in the most amazing way for the ministry He has now entrusted to me. TO GOD BE ALL THE GLORY.

To Contact:
Gerry Bezanson
Box 94
Aylesford, Nova Scotia
B0P 1C0

Lost But Not Forgotten

The Life
of
ALLAN INGRAHAM

I went onto the streets of Niagara Falls and made friends with the winos who lived in the hobo jungles, along the railway tracks in the woods by the river. I started stealing like I had been taught. Those men rode freight trains, had pots and pans hanging from trees, and a fire burning all the time. They hauled wood in and kept the fire going. Some would go downtown and panhandle for money to buy wine and rubbing alcohol. Others would panhandle for money to buy meat and food. Others would go and steal alcohol and raid gardens to get vegetables. They'd put the rubbing alcohol and wine in a big pot and mix it up. Then some would start playing guitars and mouth organs or spoons as the fire was burning and the drink was passed around. Many times the police would come in looking for people to see if there was someone there who was wanted. It was here I learned to hide and dodge the police.

I learned to be part of this crowd even as little as eight or nine years old. I would sneak away from school and go to the jungle and live with the hoboes and drink with them. I'd go out and steal for them and bring back wine, spirits and food. I'd get a pat on the back from some of the old guys and they'd say, "You're a good kid Al. You're gonna be a somebody someday. We can trust you Al". It made me feel like a million dollars, like I had a purpose and that I had some value.

I was born in Fredericton, NB on August 2, 1947. My mother was a single working lady, living with her mother. My grandfather died at the age of 42. I was a little boy living with my mother who was only 19 years old and my grandmother. There was no man around the house. I never had a dad to take me fishing or hunting or do the things that I saw other children doing. All of this made me feel different growing up.

I often wondered why I didn't have a dad. Where was my dad? Was there something different about me? Was I bad? Was I ugly? Why wasn't there a man in my life? I didn't even have a grandfather. I spent most of my time with my grandmother because my mother worked. I called my grandmother Nanny. My earliest recollections go back to her. I don't have a lot of memories of anyone else.

I was 46 years of age before I saw my biological father and he was laying in his coffin. I went through a lot of mixed feelings that day. There were half brothers and half sisters there and I was told these were my family. I felt so confused and tormented inside, I didn't know whether to laugh or cry. I couldn't do either so I just went outside and left.

Alcohol had always been the answer for me. I grew up immersed in it. I lived with my grandmother in Fredericton and then she sold her home and went to live in Niagara Falls, Ontario. I was only seven years old at this time.

Meanwhile, my mother met a man named Charlie. She began to seem different. She only had one thing on her mind and that was Charlie. Being young, I didn't understand what was happening, so I dug a deeper hole for myself and went further into the pit. I began to live in my mind.

I would go out and sit in the woods alone and dream of living on a desert island. Many times I dreamt I was the Lone Ranger, that old time cowboy who rode around with his native friend, Tonto. He wore a mask, had a gun with silver bullets, and he used to help people out of trouble. When he had helped people, he would ride off into the sunset. This was my fantasy while I sat alone by the river. Everything would be pure and happy. I would help people like my mother and grandmother. Tonto wouldn't be Tonto, he would be my dad and my partner. We would ride off together and he would pat me on the back. People would wave at me and thank me for helping them. I really wanted to help people and be a good person.

I remember the first few things my grandmother had taught me. She said, "Always be a good boy Allan". She always wanted me to be a good person. After she moved to Niagara Falls and my mother met Charlie, I began to spend most of my time alone in the woods. I liked to run through the fields and chase butterflies and race the birds. I was small, but I was fast.

When I was about six years old, my mother married Charlie. I felt rejected and spent even more time out in the woods and living in my head. I began to bad-mouth my mother. As I look back now, I guess I lost whatever attention I felt I had. There was a trickle of hope inside me that Charlie could have been my dad, but I realize now that I wasn't very easy to get along with. I was angry that I had lost my grandmother. I missed her. She was someone I could always confide in. No matter what the problem, I could go to her and she would give me a big hug and kiss and a cookie and say, "Now, now, everything is going to be alright".

After my grandmother left I started to try to build a relationship with my mother. It seemed I had failed again because I thought she had found someone more important than me. It wasn't long after they were married that they had children. I now had two brothers. That just meant there was more time taken away from me. I just felt more and more left out.

When my grandmother moved to Ontario, I realized how much I missed her. Even if she wasn't my dad, I could talk to her and confide in her. The void kept getting bigger and bigger and the loneliness and the emptiness were with me constantly. Then one day I got word that my grandmother had sent for me. She was in the Falls and had remarried a man named Bert. He had been a former boarder in her home.

Charlie and my mother had started traveling around since he was in the army, and my grandmother wanted me to live with her.

I had all these dreams and fantasies about how great it would be to live with Nanny again. This man who she married could be my new dad. He would be the new man in my life. He would take me hunting and fishing and pay attention to me.

By now, I was almost eight years old and I often wondered why I had never gone to school. I saw other boys my age going to school. I'd play with them in the summer and then they'd go back to school in the fall and I'd be left alone. I was excited about going to be with my grandmother and my new grandfather. He was my new dad as far as I was concerned. I had mixed feelings of anger and hurt towards my mom and Charlie.

My grandmother hired some relatives from Niagara Falls to go to Fredericton and bring "little Al" back to Niagara Falls. I don't have a lot of memories from my childhood, but I remember the day I arrived there. Nanny came running to me, hugged me and took me into the house. The house was a little different. It was beside a graveyard and I thought that was kind of funny. That was not how I had dreamt it. Nanny took me in to meet Bert. He was drunk when I arrived. It didn't take long for me to realize that things weren't going to be the way I had dreamed. Bert had wiry, dark curly hair, dark skin, and a flattened nose. He weighed about 200 lbs. and was 5' 10". He was an impressive, rough-looking dude. When I got near him I could smell alcohol. That seemed to be the story of Bert's life and the relationship we had over the next number of years.

I started school that year at eight. It was the first time I had ever attended school. I was very small so I was teased a lot. School was a miserable experience for me. Home was no better. The alcohol abuse and the fighting that took place there just confused me even further. Bert ruled with an iron hand. My age or size didn't matter to him. Neither did the fact that my Nanny was a woman. He abused both of us. If he didn't abuse us physically he did verbally with foul language that I'd never heard before. However I picked it up and it became part of my life.

Life didn't have any purpose or meaning other than to survive the best way I knew how. By now I began to take sips of Bert's alcohol. He'd ask me to go and pour him a drink. Then I'd take a sip. In my mind I felt that if Bert was drinking it, it must be good. I didn't really care for the taste of it. I just enjoyed the warming effect and how it made me feel bigger. I could feel myself strutting after having a few sips. I'd go and pose in front of the mirror and make faces at myself and flex my little muscles.

It wasn't long before I was watching where Bert hid his alcohol or when he had a brew on. He used to make homemade brew and sell it to his friends. There were a few friends that he hung around with regularly, and they all would make booze. The brew would take four to six days to ferment and they'd all sit around waiting for it. They drank wine and partied and talked about their great hunting and fishing trips. One of Bert's friends had a son named Ronnie who was around my age. He had four sisters.

Ronnie and I became friends and when those men got together drinking, fighting, partying, cursing and talking about naked women, we would have each other to talk to. Ronnie and I would get together and talk about our fears, hurts and pains and the things that had happened to us. We were both able to identify with slaps across the face and kicks in the backside. Bert and Ronnie's dad trained us to steal in stores. We were to steal cigarettes, food and whatever else we could. We would then sell these things for money to buy wine, while they waited for their homemade brew to be strong enough to drink. We learned where they hid that too.

When they got drunk, Ronnie and I would steal the brew. We would drink it and feel like mighty men of war. We felt like Tonto and the Lone Ranger. We would do even more daring things and take chances stealing. Ronnie taught me how to break into houses and cottages and steal stereos, tv's, tape recorders, rifles, guns and other stuff that was in summer cottages or homes around the Niagara Falls area.

Ronnie also told me that there was a great place to pick people's pockets. The perfect time was when they went swimming at the beach. Some of the people were older and we could overpower them and take their wallets right off them.

A whole new world began to open up for Ronnie and I, especially after we drank alcohol. It made us bolder and braver and not afraid. We learned how to get around Bert and Harry and others. We learned how to give them the answers they wanted to hear. It didn't matter what we told them anyway, they never believed us because there were so many lies in their own lives.

Stealing became a way of life for me. It gave me control of my life. Ronnie and I were hanging around together and Bert told me I could never do anything right. Well I showed Bert. I was doing real good. I could steal whatever I wanted and it would be mine, and it didn't matter who worked for it or how much it was worth. If I wanted it, I would go and get it. Ronnie and I would go out when all the men were passed out and my Nanny would say, "Now, now Al, don't be a bad boy. Be a good boy and don't fight or hurt anyone".

It was difficult at school because the other kids made fun of me and called me names. I couldn't hold back, so I fought with them and sometimes I would get a beating. I'd come home all bruised and Bert would beat me because I got a beating. He'd say, "I'm gonna toughen you up. I'm gonna make a man out of you. You can't do anything right". I began to believe Bert, that I couldn't do anything right and never would. He hurt me. He was the only male figure in my life and I looked up to him.

In my heart there was always hope, because once in a while, during sober times, Bert would take me fishing. I remember those days when we went fishing and I'd walk beside him and look up at him. There would be a little joy in my heart thinking that this is it; this is the turning point; this is going to happen all the time. Just as quick as it happened, it ended. Bert often broke his promises to take me fishing or hunting. Sometimes, during hunting season, he'd take me with him and let me carry the gun. I felt so good. It felt great going out into the woods with him. One time, we shot a couple of partridges and he said, "One of these day Allan, you're gonna be able to take this big 12 gauge shotgun and I'm gonna let you shoot a bird".

A few days later we were going back into the woods and Ronnie and his father had come with us. The only difference this time was that they were drinking and had a bottle with them. When we got out into the woods Bert said, "Come on Al, you can shoot this gun now. You're big enough to shoot it". And I thought, "Oh boy, this is great! I'm gonna get to shoot that big shotgun that only Bert could shoot. I'm gonna be a man. I'm gonna be like the Lone Ranger". Bert said, "Hold it up to your shoulder. Hold it a little away from your shoulder and I'll pull the hammer back for you".

He pulled the hammer back and said, "Aim at the can I put on that tree Al. You can do it. Make sure you keep the gun away from your shoulder as I pull the trigger". That space between the stock of the gun and my shoulder was filled with the impact of that 12 gauge jerking back. It hit my shoulder hard and knocked me down on the ground. My shoulder was badly bruised and I felt so hurt, sore and sad. I was upset because I couldn't believe that Bert would do that to me. Both men laughed and laughed and then they did the same thing to Ronnie.

We were both so hurt that our dreams and our expectations were ruined. I was so sad inside. Bert often made promises but didn't keep them. I wanted him to care for me. I wanted his approval at any cost but he always had a negative name for me. I used to hear him raving at my Nanny in the night when he was drunk as I lay awake on my bed. He would be calling me names and putting me down. I'd lay in my bed and look at the ceiling and pretend to be asleep. I was filled with pain inside and I wasn't able to get it out. Not one tear would come. How I ached.

Many of those nights laying in bed, I thought that if only I had a dad, then he'd come and give me a kiss and a word of encouragement and say he was proud of me. Even when Bert beat me physically I couldn't cry. The words hurt me badly inside. The beatings, the belt, and the kicks, and the punches and the slaps were so bad, but I still wouldn't cry. I'd show them all. I'd fix them. So I hit the streets.

This is when I discovered acceptance with the winos in their hobo camp down by the railroad tracks. These people in the hobo jungle gave me purpose. Some of them told me that they had spent most of their lives there and it was a pretty good life. They told us, "We travel all over Canada; we jump a freight; the tracks are our home; the box cars are our palaces; we just live life for the minute". I found out where I belonged.

Alcohol became my god; trickery my means of survival. My philosophy was take what you could at any cost. No-one cared anyway. Bert began to realize that I had money at this time. It wasn't long before he and his buddies would watch for Ronnie and I, grab us and take what money we had. It didn't matter that it was ours. It didn't matter that we had worked hard to steal it. They just took it. Then he'd say, "Go out and steal another carton of cigarettes for us and don't come back till you do or I'll smash your little face against the wall". I knew that he meant it. Ronnie and I had money stashed in our private places. Bert and his friends soon caught on to that. They'd follow us and take it. Then they'd buy more wine with it

My mind swam with anger. Oh to be six feet tall and 200 lbs! Since that wasn't possible I began to travel with a gang of older boys. I was accepted and became part of the crowd. I wanted someone to accept me. The winos weren't enough. I needed to be accepted by my peers and I wanted more power. I realized that there was power in numbers.

There were older girls in this gang and they sent me to do what they wouldn't do. Bert had taught me well. The more I stole for them, the more I felt part of the crowd. The more I felt accepted, the better I felt. I was the pro. If you wanted something Al would get it. Al and Ronnie were buddies. They were inseparable. They were partners. I did whatever I had to. I wanted to be loved. I laughed and carried on and told jokes, but on the inside I was just a little boy who felt empty inside.

One time Ronnie and I were caught by the police breaking into a school and they brought us home. I remembered hearing Ronnie screaming as his father beat him. Then he came outside and thanked the police for bringing him home. Now Ronnie and I were really angry. There were no more tears just anger. Ronnie said "I'll never cry again". I'd already made that decision years ago. No-one ever gave me the opportunity to cry. No-one had given me the opportunity to feel anything other than emptiness and loneliness. There were no hugs, no kisses, no bedtime stories. I didn't know what those things were in those days, but I now see what was lacking in my life. I see what I was longing for in the alcohol.

172

Ronnie and I decided this is it! We're going to be buds till we die. We're gonna shut down and not let anyone get to us. Soon stealing from stores just wasn't enough. It didn't satisfy us. We robbed homes and cottages. What was theirs became mine. I took it and it felt good.

One troubling situation at this time was that some of the older girls in the gang were paying attention to me. The guys would laugh about my size and joke about when I'd become a man. I didn't understand what they were talking about. I was young and I wasn't interested in women yet. I just wanted to be accepted.

Some of the older girls took me out into a barn and explored me sexually. They fondled and touched me and did things that really bothered me. I wasn't prepared for it and I didn't understand it. I didn't know what was happening. I just knew that it was a private area and there was great interest as these girls giggled and touched me. They said I was becoming a man. They thought it was cool, so I thought it was cool. It left me with some difficulties to deal with later.

When I was alone I tried not to think of this experience, or the times I had witnessed Bert doing things to my grandmother, that my eight year old mind didn't understand. What bothered me most was that Nanny would say, "No, Bert don't do that. No Bert I'm not feeling well". He never seemed to listen to her, because whatever he was doing, he didn't stop for quite a while. Often I would hear my grandmother crying after he had stopped the noises in their room. When I asked my grandmother about it she said, "Be quiet Al, you wouldn't understand".

I didn't understand a lot of things. I didn't understand why there was no-one coming to parent/teacher night with me. I didn't understand why I didn't have a dad to ruffle my head, hug me and do things with me that other boys did with their dads. I was getting to the age that I knew there was a difference between me and the other boys. Not just a difference in size or whether they were dressed better, but there was a difference. They had a parent drop them off or come to things at school. Mine never went to any of the school's functions. It was very difficult for me to stay in school at this time.

Life was a nightmare for me. Bert would beat me when I was beaten at school. I was always fighting. Because of my size, everyone made fun of me. The guys in the jungle never fought with me. They drank my wine and smoked the cigarettes I stole for them, and so did the guys and girls in the club. The money I stole I gave to them.

One time a big boy tried to pull me off the baseball team. I loved to play baseball. I could run like a rabbit. I guess it was all the experience I'd had in New Brunswick when I'd run through the fields and race the birds. I liked sports and I liked to play ball. I was a good ball player. When this big boy tried to pull me off the team I beat him real bad. From that time on I got recognition. The other kids said, "Man you're mean. You're crazy. Don't mess with Al". I beat him and punched him and kicked him. I liked the recognition. I liked the encouragement. From then on I began to hurt people because it got me attention. It had released some of the stuff that was inside of me.

I was always in trouble in school with both the teachers and other students. I was expelled for fighting, cursing and bad mouthing the teachers. I'd actually physically fight with some of the teachers. Many times I would go to school without a lunch. Nobody made me a lunch and so I'd steal other kids' lunches or money. School was not a place where I was welcomed or wanted to be.

Ronnie and I made an agreement that we would always be inseparable. Then one day I got the news. I was about eleven years old when Bert and Nanny decided to move back to New Brunswick. We were going to a place outside Fredericton called Maugerville. Bert said we were going to make a new start. He would get work in construction and he told me I would like it better there. He said it would be better for my Nanny and all of us. We'd have a little garden and we'd do lots of fishing and hunting.

A little ray of hope triggered inside me even though I didn't like the idea of leaving Ronnie. We were soul brothers so that night we went to the jungle for a walk and listened to the hoboes talking. Ronnie said, "Whatever you do Al, don't lose touch with me. I wish I could go with you. Why can't you take me Al?". I told him I couldn't because you know what Bert's like. I told him we'd stay in touch and when he was older he could come down there and we'd be buddies. We'll always be buddies and partners.

I told Ronnie that Bert said he would change. He said he was going to work and I would be able to get a little part time job and make some money. We won't have to steal any more. Who knows with Bert leaving perhaps Ronnie's dad would sober up and there won't be any need for Ronnie to steal and do the things he was doing. It might be best for all of us. That night we stayed up late just walking and talking and watching the hobo's fire. I promised Ronnie I would keep in touch.

The journey to Fredericton was no different than the journey we'd made a few years ago to Niagara Falls. Bert was loaded up on wine and all the way down, he made all these promises.

We found an older house in Maugerville and got settled in. We gradually got furniture. I had a little shed out back where I spent a lot of my time. Bert never changed. If anything he got worse. Some of his former friends and drinking buddies got together and it was the same as Niagara Falls.

One night a month after we had moved to New Brunswick, Bert got a letter. He was reading it and he said, "Hey runt, get in here. You remember your old buddy Ronnie in Niagara Falls?". How could I forget Ronnie? There were so many times since we'd been here that I'd wished he was with me. I never found anyone like Ronnie. I had met some kids around my age, eleven or twelve. Then there were some fifteen and sixteen year olds who were more into my lifestyle of drinking, fighting and partying. But I missed Ronnie. I said, "Yeah, yeah Bert, I remember Ronnie." "Well" he said, "it says here that a couple of weeks ago, Ronnie was on the streets at night and he was killed in a hit and run". My heart dropped when I heard those words.

I don't know what else he said, all I could see were his lips moving. I didn't hear a thing. I ran out of the house to my shed. I couldn't even stay there. I went running to the river trying to find some comfort. I didn't believe it was possible. Ronnie couldn't be dead. We had dreams of doing things together. We were going to be the Lone Ranger and Tonto. We wanted to be gangsters together as we grew older. We'd made promises that last night in the jungle that we would do all these things together . Now he was dead. It was really lonely. But life goes on.

Then Nanny began to get ill and I saw a difference in her. She wasn't as chipper and happy and encouraging as she used to be. She steadily seemed to lose her joy. There was a grey yellowness that came over her complexion. I asked her if she was spending too much time in the sun and wind. Sometimes I'd hear her in the washroom. I'd go in after her and there were blood stains around the toilet. I thought maybe she'd had a nosebleed. I came home early from school one day. The teachers asked me to leave because I was fighting and cursing. I had been up late the night before because Bert had been drinking and screaming with his friends. Nanny had been crying and begging them to leave and Bert just gave her a backhand. I remember hearing her sob and I couldn't sleep that night. The next day at school I was very edgy and I began to fight with the teachers.

When I got home Bert said, "Your grandmother's gone to the hospital". I said, "What's wrong with her Bert? Did you hurt her?". That was my first thought, that Bert had hurt her. "No" Bert said, "she just got real sick. She went into the washroom and was in there for a long time. I heard a noise so I went in and she had passed out on the floor. There was a lot of blood everywhere. I don't really know what happened. It's probably not too serious. You know your grandmother, she's a pretty tough person. She always bounces back. Al, you're going to have to help me around here now with the cooking and the cleaning. I can't do it all myself".

I found myself cooking for Bert and his friends and going out stealing cigarettes for them. I did try to visit my Nanny in the hospital, but it wasn't long before she was transferred from Fredericton to St. John. I don't know why they took her that far away. Nobody seemed to know anything. Nobody wanted to tell me anything. I didn't know what was going on. I just knew my Nanny wasn't here any more. Bert wasn't a whole lot of help. He was meaner and angrier than before.

During this time, Bert told me he had just found out about a long-lost daughter he had in Montreal. He told me that while my grandmother was in the hospital, he was going to visit her. Bert left for Montreal and was gone quite a few days. I was in charge of the house. I was all alone. I went back to school again for a while but it was a touchy situation.

After about a week Bert landed back. I smelled alcohol on his breath. "Bon jour" he said, "I brought back my French daughter from Montreal". He introduced his daughter to me. It seemed funny the way Bert and his daughter carried on. I'd never seen fathers kissing their daughters on the lips, or putting their hands on their backsides, or rubbing their hands down the inside of their legs. It left me with some strange questions in my mind. She was cute and pretty, but she didn't look much like Bert.

Nanny was still in the hospital and Bert didn't go to visit her. Late one night I woke up and heard noises coming from downstairs. It was dark and I saw a light on. I snuck out of my bed and went creeping down the stairs. Bert's daughter screamed, "Bert there's someone watching". They were both naked on the couch. I thought what kind of way was that for someone to treat their daughter. I really didn't understand. Bert came running after me and punched and slapped me. He told me that I was snooping. I knew I was in trouble, but I didn't know why.

The next day the daughter left and I never saw her or heard from her again. We never talked about it. Bert just said, "Look you scared my daughter away. You're no good for anything. She's gone because of you". I wondered what was wrong with me.

One day I was in town and when I arrived home Nanny was there. She had lost a lot of weight. Bert told me I would have to help my grandmother around the house a lot now because she had a bag on her side. They did some kind of operation to save her. My Nanny wasn't that kind of a person. She'd keep working and give me a rub on the head every now and again and say, "Al you be a good boy now". I tried but it was hard. I was so mixed up.

I didn't have many friends outside of the house. I fought with most of them at school. There were a few guys that I hung out with, but no-one could ever replace Ronnie. One night I was sleeping and I heard the noises that I had heard before saying, "No Bert, no Bert, please, no Bert". Bert didn't stop. Afterwards I heard my Nanny crying and saying to Bert that he had really hurt her. The next day she was bent over even more. A couple of days later she went back to the hospital and that was the last time I saw my Nanny alive.

Bert stayed drunk through the funeral and the wake. My mother and Charlie came and they were all angry at Bert. I quit school at this time in Grade 7. There was little purpose in going to school. I wasn't learning much and I wasn't very respectful. If anyone asked me to do anything, I rebelled against their authority. I didn't want anyone telling me what to do. I was fed up with my life. Stealing, drinking alcohol and smoking cigarettes was a lot easier. I became very rude to the teachers. I spit at them and finally they gave me a choice at 15 years of age, to quit school on my own or they would have me removed. They suggested that the best thing would be to quit.

At 15 years of age, having not completed Grade 7 and weighing only 90 lbs, I quit school. I worked at different jobs such as dish washer, construction and hotel work. I was just trying to make a few bucks but unable to do anything legitimate. My state with Bert wasn't a very good one. I didn't listen to his authority either. We fought and argued a lot and I thought it was time to start moving on.

I stayed with Bert for another month after the funeral. Then he really got violent and told me I was nothing but a little bastard, a sawed-off runt and I was good for nothing. I couldn't take it any more. I decided I was history and I left.

The next couple of years I moved around from place to place, drinking and partying. I stayed at friends' homes whenever the opportunity arose but I constantly wore out my welcome. Then I would hit the streets. I drank, stole, robbed and worked a little. I applied for a job at the Mactaquac Dam, a project in Fredericton. I got a job as a kitchen helper, but I got back into the booze and didn't show up for work. I wore out my welcome everywhere I went.

On the odd occasion, I made a visit to Charlie and Mom's. I used to look at Charlie in his army uniform and wondered why I hadn't stayed with them. So I went to live with Charlie, Mom and and my brothers for a while. Maybe if I had stayed there and Charlie had gotten me that job at the Bowling Alley where I could have made a few bucks, I would have been okay. I still felt that I didn't fit in with any of them. At least there wasn't the same screaming that took place when I lived with Bert. Even though Charlie drank, he was very quiet and a gentleman. I kept wondering what would have happened if I had stayed with them.

I just kept on partying and drinking and many times when I visited Charlie and Mom, I'd look at their home and see that they did have some peace and comfort. Charlie did influence me with his career in the service and I began to think that it could be the answer. Maybe if I join the army, I'll become a great general or soldier and find my fortune and my place in life. I mentioned this to Juanita.

She was a young girl I had known since the time she was eleven or twelve, and I was a little bit older. We used to date and I talked to Juanita about it. She said, "Why don't you just stop drinking. You're so angry all the time". I told her I wasn't angry, that was just the way it was. She lived with her parents and family.

I would trick her dad into driving her into town because they lived outside the city. We heard about a man named Billy Graham and he'd come to town doing crusades. I'd tell her dad that we were going to the crusade so her dad would drive her into town. Then we'd run off for the evening and have fun together. Juanita was a bright spot in my otherwise confused and troubled life. I confided in Juanita quite a bit. She was worried about me. I talked to her about the army and she thought that it might be good for me.

I talked to Charlie and Mom about it. I was only 17 years old and had no purpose in life. I thought maybe I could be a famous general some day. Charlie and my mother had to sign for me to enlist because I was only 17. In the back of my mind I thought, at least in the army I could legally drink at 18. I had heard there were lots of alcohol and parties in the army.

I enlisted at the Gagetown Camp outside of Fredericton, NB. Shortly after that I was on a plane in uniform. I'll never forget the day I got my uniform. I posed in the mirror and saluted myself. I felt like I belonged. It wasn't long before I was in Calgary going through basic training. It wasn't like I had thought it would be. There were a lot of rules, and I didn't like rules. I didn't like having to listen to Sergeants and people in authority over me. However, I did manage to get through basic. It was marching and doing all kinds of drills. I was up early in the morning and into bed early at night.

When we got leave, we'd go into town and drink and party. I wasn't old enough nor did I look old enough, because of my size, to get into bars. I would drink on the streets with the native people, the Cree, and my other army friends who weren't old enough to drink. We'd get the older guys to go to the liquor store and buy us alcohol. Then we'd drink it on the streets and at other people's houses.

I finally finished my six month basic training and thought, now I'm going to get a break and get into the battalion and get assigned to a post. Everyone said I'd be going to Wainwright, Alberta. I'd heard that they used real bullets down there. Then I began to hear that I might have to go to Cyprus. That didn't appeal to me because I thought that would be real war. They were shooting people over there. I could be one of those who could get killed. That wasn't my plan. I didn't join the army to go to Cyprus and get shot.

So I spent more time in town than at the base, until finally I was on the run and reported AWOL by the army. I owed a lot of money to different men in the battalion. I had borrowed money for drinks and told them I would pay them back. The threat of Cyprus and these unpaid debts made it easier to walk away. This was not how it was meant to be. After all, there were too many orders and too many people telling me what to do in the army. I didn't like it at all.

After six months they found me and took me back. I was dismissed from the army and headed to Edmonton. I was partying and drinking on the streets and hanging around the race tracks where I met some famous horsemen. I began to work with horses and train thoroughbreds. It became another way of life for me. I enjoyed it. I was small so I was good for something. I was also at a training track outside Winnipeg for a time. I worked under a man named Cap Harris. He was one of the best trainers in Canada. He'd trained a lot of the famous jockeys. Here the same thing happened, more booze, more partying, and more night life.

Then I moved to a little town in Saskatchewan where I was training and had a promising career. My career didn't mean anything to me. Booze took first place. I wanted to drown out the pain and the loneliness. I didn't seem to fit in with people who didn't drink. I always felt they were making fun of me and when I drank I didn't care.

I hitch-hiked back to Alberta from Saskatchewan. I was picked up by a lot of weird people wanting to do weird things. Sometimes I would lead them on for their booze and then rob them, which kept me in spending money. I ended up back in Edmonton where I continued partying and drinking with my friends, the Cree. I was living in alleys and run-down places. Many times, we were so desperate from drinking booze, shaving lotion and rubbing alcohol, that we didn't have the nerve to go and steal, so we'd trap pigeons from peoples' barns. We take stuff from their gardens and then cook the pigeons to make a meal.

I lived with the Cree in the streets of Edmonton and sometimes in their homes. They finally got fed up with me after I fought and beat up a couple of their family members over some booze. They threw me out and I found myself alone again. By now I was desperate. I had no place to go. The flop houses didn't want me any more either.

So I turned myself in because I had no place to stay and I had no food. I was wanted on some old charges, thefts and break and enters. When I was put in Fort Saskatchewan Prison outside of Edmonton they weighed me. I had dropped from 90 lbs. to 70 lbs. My face was sunken in. I was a mess and I was sick. Prison really turned out to be a place of rescue. I got three meals, a cot, some tobacco and some attention. I began to build up my body again. I had some place to sleep and began to feel a bit better.

After six months I was sent from Fort Saskatchewan to a bush prison camp up north. I served some time in the bush camp doing different jobs. I was eating well and the fresh air was wonderful. I felt my strength coming back. The odd time we'd make a little brew, have a party and talk about the things we were going to do when we got out; the scores we were going to make, and the people we were going to rob. Those nights I'd lay awake and realize there were a lot of people around me but I was still lonely.

I often thought of my Nanny and how she told me to be a good boy and not to fight. I even thought about old Bert. I remembered how he took me fishing and hunting once in a while. I even thought about the time Bert made me drink hot blood out of the deer he shot. He hung it up and he drank a cup of hot blood. He cut the deer's throat and the blood dripped into a can and he told me, I had to drink it because it would make me a man. I remember the red sticky blood on my face and lips and the sweet warm taste of it. I thought, "that's not so bad after all. Bert's a man. He's a big burly guy and I wanted to be like Bert". And I remembered those things as I lay in my prison cell.

I thought about Juanita and how Charlie and Mom were doing. There was no peace or contentment as I lay there and listened to the other men sleeping. I could hear one man sneaking from his bed into another man's bed. I could hear some of those same noises that Nanny used to make. I heard young boys saying, "no, no, no" as older men came to their beds and now I knew what was going on. In that world, you didn't interfere or get involved.

As my days grew shorter at the bush camp I anticipated leaving and yet part of me didn't want to leave. It was a place I belonged; where I fit in. I had my meals and some comfort. I didn't have to worry about stealing pigeons, or raiding gardens, or breaking into someone's home. I felt I could stay, but I also wanted to get out and set out on my course in life.

When I was released, I met a friend in Calgary who had a tire changing business. We realized that there was a lot of money to be made selling tires off the big transport trucks. So with his equipment and truck we began a great business of selling stolen transport tires. We did well and partied a lot.

Around this time I was hanging around with a couple of bikers and we partied and dealt drugs. One young girl, Dot, stood out in my mind. She was a pill popper who liked pot and hash. You could tell she wanted to be accepted. She was always rubbing up against some guy, especially the ones with the dope. Many times you'd see her being led off into a room or the back seat of a car. She would come back in smiling and laughing and you could tell she was high.

One night we were at a party. There was lots of dope smoking and people were passing pills around. Dot was dancing on the tables and enjoying herself. A little while later she disappeared. That was par for the course so nobody thought anything of it. Later that night someone tried to get into the washroom but the door was locked. They thought someone must be passed out in there. They shouldered the door through. I was in right behind them and there, in a pool of blood, in the bathtub was Dot. She got fed up with life. She couldn't take being passed from man to man. She'd survived every day with drugs and finally had enough. After filling the bathtub with water, she sat in the tub and watched as it filled with her blood. It was the reality of another life gone. I just got out of there and I disappeared.

I tried to pull the blinds down in my life. I didn't want to see any more death. I'd seen my grandmother dying. I'd seen others die and I'd lost Ronnie. Now here was Dot, dead, in a sea of blood with staring eyes looking at the ceiling. It was all over drugs and pills. I hitch-hiked to Vancouver. I had a few bucks from my friend that I had worked with in Calgary. He gave me a front to go out there.

I arrived there and got established near the Granville Street Mall, around Davis and Hastings Street and Pigeon Park. Before long I met up with a guy who set me up dealing hash and pot. I sat around with the hookers and saw the mascara running down their faces; getting out of cars; some times slapped around by their johns and even getting slapped around by their pimps who took the money to buy more heroin. I saw the lost and empty look in these girls' eyes. I watched them stumble down alleys and fall over drunks as they lay passed out. That was the story of my life, flop houses, cheap rooms, drinking, and stealing.

It was a fast life. I got busted dealing drugs. I was charged with accessory. This was after I had left Vancouver and headed to Calgary again. During that time I hooked up with my biker buddies. We were partying it up and carrying on just like we had the night Dot died. Nobody talked about Dot. Nobody remembered Dot. Nobody ever brought up her name. Dot was history!

You didn't bring up the past in those days. I didn't talk about Ronnie, but I did think about him. If I had only been there, perhaps Ronnie wouldn't have been hit and killed. He was out stealing that night and I believed that if I had been there he wouldn't be dead now. Dot was dead, so was Nanny and Fredericton was history. Juanita was thousands of miles away. I was a failure in the army. Training horses didn't work out either.

One time I was at this place with my biker buddies and we were partying and doing the same things that we always did. Someone tapped me on the shoulder and said, "Hey Al, see that guy over there, he's a rat, he's an informant. He put the finger on some of the boys. We'll hafta do something about that Al". I said, "Don't worry about it, I'll take care of it". It wasn't long before my buddies and I were charged with attempted murder.

The trial went on for eight months. We were let out on our own recognizance. They trusted us with bail. The man was badly beaten and ended up in the hospital. I was the number one suspect, but I had an alibi that night. I had witnesses that said I was somewhere else. Finally, after many months, the guy that had us charged was declared an unfit witness during the course of the trial. He was picked up and charged with robberies and break and enters, so he became a non-credible witness against us. The case was thrown out. I left the court room with a smile on my face. I laughed because I had beaten them again. I partied around the city for the next while and laughed and talked about my conquest. Life didn't have any real meaning. I took what I wanted and I got what I wanted and that's the way I liked it. At least I thought I did.

I left Vancouver because it was getting hot. The cops were wise to me. They were watching me. Wherever I was, they showed up. I had a few bucks in my pocket and took off for Toronto. I met a lot of funny people on the way. They offered me all kinds of things, drugs, alcohol and favours. I robbed many of them. They were too afraid to report me to the police because of the kinds of things they wanted to do with me. I headed to Toronto and partied all the way.

I dropped into Sudbury and drank with the hard rock miners for a while. I finally made it to Toronto. I hit the parks on Queen Street, Parliament Street and Shuter Street and down around that area. I met up with an old buddy I hadn't seen for a while who had a tow truck business. I stayed with him and his family, but kept on stealing and robbing. One night I passed out. I woke up to find my money was all gone and I accused him of taking it. He denied it and I thought he was lying to me and I beat him real bad. The family didn't want me to live with them any more, even though I said I was sorry.

I ended up around the Allan Gardens area. Sometimes I got a free flop and a sandwich at Seaton House. I slept in parks and cars. I did whatever was necessary to survive on the streets. The Old Duke Tavern became my place of refuge. I'd go from table to table getting free beers. It got to the point that there was nothing left for me in Toronto. I'd been picked up by the police a few times. I'd spent a few nights in the drunk tank and the Don Jail. I'd also been picked up for vagrancy, so I headed out.

I was about 20 years old when I hitch-hiked back to Fredericton. I stayed with some friends for a while and then went to stay at Charlie and my Mom's. I finally got a job in construction and stayed at it for a while. I was still drinking, partying and living it up. Charlie and Mom didn't go for that.

I was glad to see Juanita. She was 17, and soon we got together again. In a couple of months we realized we were going to have a child. We decided we would get married. I went to Juanita's father and said, "Mr. Bennett, I want to marry your daughter. I want to look after her and care for her". Mr. Bennett gave us his blessing as did her mother. There was a reception at the house with booze and partying. Juanita knew this was my last night of drinking. I wasn't going to drink any more. I was going to sober up, get a job, go to work, and look after the little baby that was growing inside of her. I made all these plans and promises and we both believed I would do it.

We stayed at her parents' house for a while and then we got our own little house. I didn't have a job. I was on welfare and we started fighting. I was drinking and doing the things I had always done before. Juanita said, "You promised". I'd just say, "Oh give me a break". She'd leave and go to her parent's house, then she'd come back and I'd make all the promises again.

My first son was born and he was a beautiful boy and I loved him. I didn't know what to do with him. I only knew how to drink. I didn't even know how to hold him. Unable to express myself, Juanita left again. I took off and hitch-hiked to Oshawa, Ontario. I'll get a job and look after my wife and son. I just couldn't deal with all these things at once.

I got a job at E. P. Taylor's farm working with horses. It was good for a while but I ended up getting fired from there for drinking. I got another job, made some money and sent it to Juanita for her and the baby to come up on the train. I had written and told her I had a job and an apartment. I did have the apartment but I was on welfare again. I was also drinking heavily again. Juanita was going through the same trauma as before and she didn't like it. She had relatives in that area and from time to time she'd move out and stay with them. I'd go over and fight with her and fight with them. I actually got into a fist fight with her uncle one day. I'd convince her to come back and she did. Then we found out that she was pregnant with our second child. Juanita gave birth to a lovely baby girl. Here I was, a husband and father with two children. I was overwhelmed, I didn't know what to do. The only thing I knew how to do was drink and I did, lots of it. There was more fighting with Juanita.

I couldn't be around her or the children so I left and hitch-hiked back to Fredericton. I stayed with Charlie and my mother for a time. While I was there they saved up enough money for Juanita to come back with the children. It was the same thing again....more drinking, more fighting, more promises. Here we were with two children living in a rat infested house. I tried to work. I worked at Pyramid Homes for a while. I got laid off there and went to York Steel. Then I got laid off there and went back to Pyramid Homes. Nothing changed. In the end, Juanita just threw her hands up in the air and gave up.

After an especially violent evening when I chased her around the house and tried to abuse her, she took the children and left. When I came home the next day the place was empty. She went home to her parent's and I wasn't allowed there.

I kept on drinking. Then I got accepted in Moncton for a school upgrading course. I realized I had to get some schooling. I wanted to become a bricklayer. I went to Manpower and they put me in a course in Moncton. I relocated and tried to make a new start. Then I found out Juanita was pregnant with our third child. I wanted to help but there was nothing much I could do. I was in school and I was going to make it this time. I was going to get my high school education and I'd become a bricklayer. Then we'd have a proper home and be a family, and I'd be able to take my boys hunting and fishing and look after my little girl. I was going to be the Lone Ranger again. I was going to do the right thing. I was going to give Juanita what she really deserved.

I hadn't been at at school long before it became stressful and I couldn't concentrate, so I started drinking again. Then I got word that Juanita was in the hospital giving birth to our baby. I immediately hitch-hiked to Fredericton and went to the hospital. When I got there the Mounties were there and they stopped me from going into the hospital to see her and my new baby son. I was turned away from the hospital so I went back to Moncton.

I forgot about school and being a brick layer. I got involved with some serious men who had served time in Dorchester and other penitentiaries. Some are in prison today with life sentences. It was the same old story, partying and drug dealing. One time I went to Fredericton to sell some drugs. I did some break and enters and got arrested. I was in and out of court for a while, but was finally convicted and sentenced to one year in the Old York County Jail in Fredericton. It was a secure place and one of the oldest jails in Canada. It was a dungeon type jail and it was rough. While I was there I ended up stabbing a guy over some food. I was angry and miserable and drank brew and partied it up as much as I could.

While I was in there, word came to me that old Bert had been found in the St. John River, behind the Riverview Arms where he used to go to drink. He was dead and had been in the water for a few days. Bert was in his fifties by now and nobody knew for sure how he died. They thought he was coming from the bootlegger's in his boat and being drunk, he probably tipped over. Bert couldn't swim, so he drowned. I felt something, but I don't really know what it was. I was not allowed to go to his funeral so I wrecked my cell.

That night I was laying on the floor of my cell and remembered old Bert and the night the police brought me home. They were going to charge me and Bert covered up for me. He did take me hunting once in a while and I remembered the good things. I remembered the last time I had seen old Bert. He had remarried and had a family. I went to visit and Bert was just the same, drinking and treating his new wife and family the way he treated Nanny and me. That was the last time I saw him. I laid in my cell that night and I think, in some strange way, I missed him.

I did my time and got out of jail and headed for Toronto.

For almost 20 years I never saw my children. I moved around Toronto and lived with different people and took odd jobs. I slept on the streets and flopped at different places. I did what I could to exist. My life kept getting worse. The older I got, the more I bottomed out. The more I bottomed out, the more I'd party. It was a vicious cycle. I did drugs and I dealt drugs. Everything started to catch up with me. The people I knew in Toronto didn't have any faith in me. If they went to sleep I would rob them. I was a survivor. I was mad at everyone.

I remember sitting in Allan Gardens and a young woman, a bit younger than me, came up and sat with me and began to talk about my life. I told her I had no place to stay and was hungry and she told me that God loved me. I'd never heard that before. I remember one time Bert's mother came for a visit and she talked about God loving her, and she had all these little beads and statues she carried around with her. She seemed really different to me. Yet here this girl was telling me that God loves me. I didn't understand that too much. How could God love anyone like me? If God did love me why did I have to go through all this stuff?

She said, "Why don't you come to my house, meet my parents and have something to eat". I went to her home and her parents seemed very nice and kind. They had some of the same kind of statues that Bert's mother had but they weren't like her. They didn't seem as mysterious and weird as Bert's mom. They gave me a nice meal and there was a warm atmosphere in their home. They wanted me to go to church with them that night. I wasn't ready for church at that time.

I knew there was a God. I just had to look around and see the sun, moon, stars, trees, rivers and the beauty of mountains and I knew there was a God. I didn't know anything about church. The only thing I did know was that many times I would stand outside churches in Toronto panhandling to get money for food. People turned up their noses at me when they were coming out of church. I thought if they were such wonderful people why didn't they give me a little cash. I didn't want anything to do with churches. I just wanted to be back where I knew the turf. I figured that there must be a trick with this family. Why else would they be so kind to me. I told them no and said thanks for the food and headed back to my park bench.

I knew the area, the street, and I knew the people. I was one of them. I drifted around Toronto and then went to Niagara Falls. I didn't work and wasn't on welfare, I just stole or begged and when people would take me in, I slept there. Sometimes I'd get a meal at a soup kitchen. During this time, I made the odd trip back to Fredericton. I was dealing drugs to get money to travel with. I knew where Juanita was living, so on one occasion I went by. I saw my boys. They recognized me from a picture and they took off and ran back to their mother. They didn't want anything to do with me.

I hitch-hiked back to Ontario and kept living that no-purpose lifestyle. It was getting harder because the park benches were getting colder as I got older. It was getting harder to make a living and finally in 1988, I got totally fed up with Toronto and decided to go back to Fredericton. I had been working with a guy doing some drug dealing and some brick laying. He got tired of me making a mess around his house and he gave me money, in payment for some of the work I had done. I got on a train at Union Station, picked up some booze and headed east.

I arrived in Fredericton after a couple of days of partying, singing and hanging out with the "Newfies" going home after working in Ontario. When I got off the train I found out that Juanita was working at her sister's restaurant. I went there but her sister and mother were there. I ordered some booze and they asked me to leave. I went to a local bar in Fredericton, got drunk and slept on the St. John Riverbank that night. The next day I went down to local businesses and stole jackets and sold them to get more money to drink.

One night I met a taxi driver who was an old friend of mine and I thought great, he would take me home. Instead he told me about the Fredericton Emergency Shelter where I could stay. He took me to the shelter and I hit rock bottom. My friends had deserted me. My wife and children didn't want anything to do with me. I really had no family. The people I partied with and drank with didn't want anything to do with me. I was alone!

I was now staying at the Shelter but I was still doing drugs, alcohol and rubbing alcohol. I was also eating magic mushrooms. At the shelter I met two guys and I started hanging with them and we became close friends. We smoked, drank, partied, and felt miserable. We were mad at everyone and we laughed at the business men we robbed. One day, I had just eaten a bunch of magic mushrooms, when the director of the shelter, Rev. Jim Lewis started talking to me. I was starting to get high on the mushrooms and he asked me if I'd like to go to a meeting that night. I thought it may be an AA meeting and I may meet someone who will give me a few bucks. So I agreed to go.

We went to a hotel in Fredericton. It wasn't an AA meeting but it was what I called a "Holy Roller" meeting. The only experience I'd had with anything like that was the girl in the park and Bert's mother with all her statues. Jim told me it was a Full Gospel Businessmen's Fellowship. It was a bunch of businessmen who come together and have a meeting. I thought, businessmen, maybe I can really score some money off these guys. Christmas was coming and I thought about gifts for Juanita and the kids. What have I got to lose? The mushrooms were kicking in and I was enjoying the buzz. Supper was served and I enjoyed that. Then there was some nice music and singing about God. I was tapping my foot and thinking those were good mushrooms.

Something was happening to me. I didn't understand it. People were happy and smiling. There was no booze. My belly was bulging when I finished eating. Then I heard some testimonies of people whose lives had been changed. I always knew there was a God. Then the main speaker came on and told how God had changed his life. I was looking around and saw a man in a wheelchair. Then the offer came to go forward for prayer. They said "God wants to bless and touch you". It was like I was watching one of those TV movies. People started falling down on the floor and I thought, "Boy there is some goofy thing going on here". I figured that they had been told they would get money from this guy if they fell on the floor.

Then I saw the guy in the wheel chair go up and I thought, this is where the guy gets out of the wheel chair. He got up to the front and handed the speaker a pack of cigarettes. I was stunned. It wasn't to get out of the chair, he just wanted to throw the cigarettes away. The man prayed for him. I was getting some funny feelings. Part of me wanted to run and part of me wanted to stay. I thought the mushrooms were working on me. I didn't know what was going on. I'd never seen such happy people in all my life. I'd never been around people like this. I didn't have to worry about people digging in my pockets or worry about what they wanted from me.

Then Jim asked me if I would like to go up for prayer and I thought, "Hmm, I'd like to maybe get out of here". He encouraged me and said he would go with me if I would like to have prayer. I went up and thought that the guy would offer me money too, if I fell like those others did. I had seen him whispering in some of their ears and touching them very gently and I thought, "I betcha he's gonna do that to me". So I went up and Jim stood by me. The man was Ralph Marachini. He laid his hand on the back of my neck, touched my head and said, "God I ask you to bless this man". A peace went through me that I had never experienced before. There was peace, calm and love. It was something I had never felt before. I was so relaxed.

Then he asked me if I would like to give my life to Jesus Christ. With mixed emotions, I prayed after him, "Lord Jesus, forgive my every sin. Lord I ask you right now to come into my life and take control, to be my Lord and Saviour, in Jesus name". That night God became real to me, on a personal level. My life was changed. I met a man who said, "I want to be your friend". That night, in all the confusion, I heard a voice speaking to me and He said, "I love you". I looked at Jim and said, "What?". He said, "I didn't say anything". A little while later I heard the voice say, "I put no conditions". Again I asked Jim if he said anything. He said no, but asked me if I'd heard a voice. He told me to say these words if I heard the voice again, "Here am I Lord". Sure enough I heard the voice again and I repeated what Jim had told me. Then Jesus Christ became real. I later learned that God spoke to Samuel in the Bible in the same way.

The man at the front prayed for me. He didn't give me any money but he gave me something I had never experienced in my life. I was afraid. I had mixed emotions. The businessmen gathered around me and said, "We're going to see you again". Bob and his wife took me to their home and kept their word. I thought everyone was like those people who looked down on me as they came out of their church, but these people kept their word.

They got me from the shelter, took me to their home and I had Christmas with them there. They even had gifts for me. There was another Christian man there and he was dressed up like Santa Claus. I got to sit on Santa's knee for the first time in my life. It was a beautiful Christmas. Jim Lewis turned out to be one of the Pastors at Smythe Street Cathedral and I began to attend there. Miraculously I never smoked cigarettes again, after smoking two or three packs a day before. I never drank alcohol, did drugs or stole again. God set me free. I began to know God's love and mercy.

As we went to the church I met a lot of people and one, in particular, Monty Lewis (no relation to Jim Lewis). He had also been in prison. He had been a drug addict and an alcoholic and was now heading up the prison ministry called "Cons For Christ". We became friends and we'd pray for one another. I began to grow in God's grace and His love. Monty gave me the pick of a Bible and I picked the biggest, blackest, leather bound Bible that I could find. I began to read and study it everywhere I went. I started to do volunteer work around the church such as cleaning. Then they got me a grant through Manpower so that I could get a job as the church custodian. I began to meet godly people. I was encouraged by Jim to be baptised in water (an outward sign of an inner change) as the Scriptures instruct us. I was baptised and God continued to work in my life.

God spoke to me again and told me to contact Juanita. I called her and we talked. A little later we went out for coffee, then we started seeing each other. God began to bless us as we grew towards each other. I would visit her but my children still had a problem with me. I understood how they felt because I wasn't around for them. They were upset. My oldest son was in Ontario at the time. I found out the Christmas I was at the shelter that my youngest son had heard that I was on the streets. He came looking for me to make sure I had a place to stay for Christmas. He didn't want me to be alone.

These things touched my heart. Juanita and I began to see each other regularly. Shortly after that my daughter moved to Ontario. I got my own place. I continued to work at Smythe Street Cathedral and my grant was extended. I began to do volunteer work with "Cons for Christ". I did whatever I could to help the ministry.

Alan and Juanita's first marriage

Enjoying married life – 1998.
(Re-married – Dec. 1990)

As my relationship with Juanita grew I asked her to forgive me for all the things I had done and for not being there for her. After being divorced for 20 years, Juanita and I were remarried on December 30, 1990. I thank God for a wonderful wife. God is also restoring my relationship with my children. My daughter has named her baby, Allan. A miracle in itself, for I was once the father she despised. I was also blessed to be able to take part in my oldest son's wedding.

It hasn't been an easy road, but it has been worth the extra effort. God continued to do a lot of restoration in my life. I was able to have the hurts of my life healed by attending the Overcomers 12 Step Group. It is a Bible-based drug and alcohol group, designed to help people overcome their problems with the abuse they have suffered, and to find forgiveness in Jesus. I became secure in Jesus and in myself. I'm never alone now (Matthew 28:20) for Jesus lives in me. I am God's son (John 1:12) and I belong to the family of God. This begins with my local church family, but includes all those who have believed in Jesus around the world.

I was asked to become the Community Chaplain for ex-offenders here in Fredericton by "Cons for Christ Prison Ministry". This required me to take studies in Community Corrections at St. Stephen University. On April 29, 2000 I graduated from the course with a diploma. I never completed school but God gave me the strength and perseverence to complete these studies.

Juanita and I have now been married for 11 years. We have our own home on a few acres of land in the country. My wife works as custodian at Smythe Street Cathedral. It is wonderful to be able to spend time together.

Each day I depend on God to help me be the kind of man that He wants me to be. I work with the food bank ministry of "Cons for Christ", which is now called "Bridges of Canada". It supplies food to other community chaplains for ex-offenders throughout the province of New Brunswick. We encourage families of inmates and help them with food.

We help inmates on their release from prison. We visit and minister in both federal and provincial institutions. As a matter of fact, I became the chaplain for the New Brunswick Department of Public Safety at the very jail where I had served time. We work with the government to help young

*Graduation – April 2000 – St. Stephen University –
Diploma – Community Corrections*

offenders so that they will not have to go to prison. As a Community Chaplain I now head up an Overcomer's 12 Step Group and have been able to help and counsel others.

God can change anybody's life. You can know freedom from sin and addiction ... it's your choice. Remember, Jesus loves you and you can make it.

Contact:
Allan Ingraham
c/o Bridges of Canada
Box 3414, Stn. B
Fredericton, N.B.
E3A 5H2

Peace with God

1. To have peace with God is an extraordinary event in a person's life. The first step is to become acquainted with God's plan of salvation which brings a person complete peace.

God loves you and wants you to have peace and eternal life.

The Bible says:

"...We have peace with God through our Lord Jesus Christ." (Romans 5:1)

"For God so loved the world, that he gave His only begotten Son, that whosoever believeth in Him should not perish but have everlasting life." (John 3:16)

"...I am come that they might have life, and that they might have it more abundantly." (John 10:10)

God wants man to have peace and an abundant life, but many people live their lives in such a way that does not bring them peace.

2. Man must realize his *problem of separation from God.* God created man in His own image and likeness and gave him a wonderful life. God did not make man a robot which would automatically love God, involuntarily fulfilling His will. God gave man a free choice between good and evil.

Mankind chose for itself the path of disobedience to God and lives without God. Man always had and even now has the power of choosing between good and evil. Choosing the evil way leads to *separation* from God.

MAN	GOD
(sinful)	(Holy)

The Bible says:

"For all have sinned and come short of the glory of God." (Romans 3:23)

196

"For the wages of sin is death; but the gift of God is eternal life through Jesus Christ our Lord." **(Romans 6:23)**

Throughout the ages mankind has unsuccessfully endeavoured to bridge this gulf which separates him from God.

MAN (sinful)	good works	GOD (Holy)
	religion	
	philosophy	
	morals	

In this world there exists only one solution to this problem of separation from God.

3. Acknowledge *God's way – The Cross of Calvary*

Jesus Christ is the only way out of this disastrous situation of separation from God. This separation lies as a gulf between God and man. Christ gave Himself over in order to liberate us. He died on the cross, but through His resurrection from the dead He bridged the gulf between God and man. His death and resurrection gives new life to all of those who believe in Him.

MAN (sinful)	CHRIST	GOD (Holy)

God stands on one side of this gulf and all mankind on the other. Jesus Christ, the God-man, is the bridge over this terrifying gulf and His intercession renews the broken union between God and man.

The Bible says:

"But God commendeth His love toward us, in that, while we were yet sinners, Christ died for us."

(Romans 5:8)

"Jesus saith unto him, I am the way, the truth and the life: no man cometh unto the Father, but by me." (John 14:6)

"For by grace are ye saved through faith; and that not of yourselves: it is the gift of God: Not of works, lest any man should boast." (Ephesians 2:8-9)

God provides for us the *only way*. Every person must decide for himself what he will do with Christ.

4. You must now make your decision: accept or reject Jesus Christ. We have to trust Christ and personally accept Him into our heart.

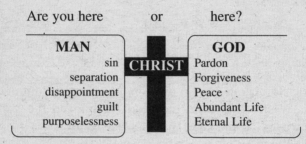

Are you here   or   here?

MAN	CHRIST	GOD
sin		Pardon
separation		Forgiveness
disappointment		Peace
guilt		Abundant Life
purposelessness		Eternal Life

The Bible says:

"Behold I stand at the door and knock: if any man hear my voice, and open the door, I will come in to him, and will sup with him, and he with Me." (Revelation 3:20)

"But as many as received Him, to them gave He power to become the sons of God; even to them that believe on His name." (John 1:12)

"That if thou shalt confess with thy mouth the Lord Jesus and shalt believe in thine heart that God hath raised Him from the dead, thou shalt be saved." (Romans 10:9)

What is stopping you from now accepting Jesus Christ as your personal Saviour?

What you must do:

1. Acknowledge that you are a sinner.

2. Repent.

3. Believe, that Christ died for you on the cross and rose from the dead.

4. Accept Christ as your personal Saviour.

How to pray:

Dear Lord,

I know that I am a lost sinner and need Your forgiveness for my sins. I believe that You died for my sins. I want to stop sinning and ask you to come into my heart and change my life. I believe that You are my Saviour and Lord, and desire to praise You together with other members of Your Church.

God's guarantee of salvation is in His Word:

Did you pray this prayer?

The Bible says:

"For all who call upon the name of the Lord shall be saved." **(Romans 10:13)**

Did you ask Christ to become your Lord and Saviour? In what kind of state do you now find yourself?

The Bible says:

"He that hath the Son hath life; and he that hath not the Son of God hath not life. These things have I written unto you that believe on the name of the Son of God; that ye may know that ye have eternal life, and that ye may believe on the name of the Son of God." **(1 John 5:12,13)**

DECISION CARD

Being convinced that I am a guilty, lost sinner, and believing that Christ died for my sins, and rose again from the dead for me, I now receive Him as my personal Saviour, and with His help, I WILL confess Him before men.

Name _____

Date _____